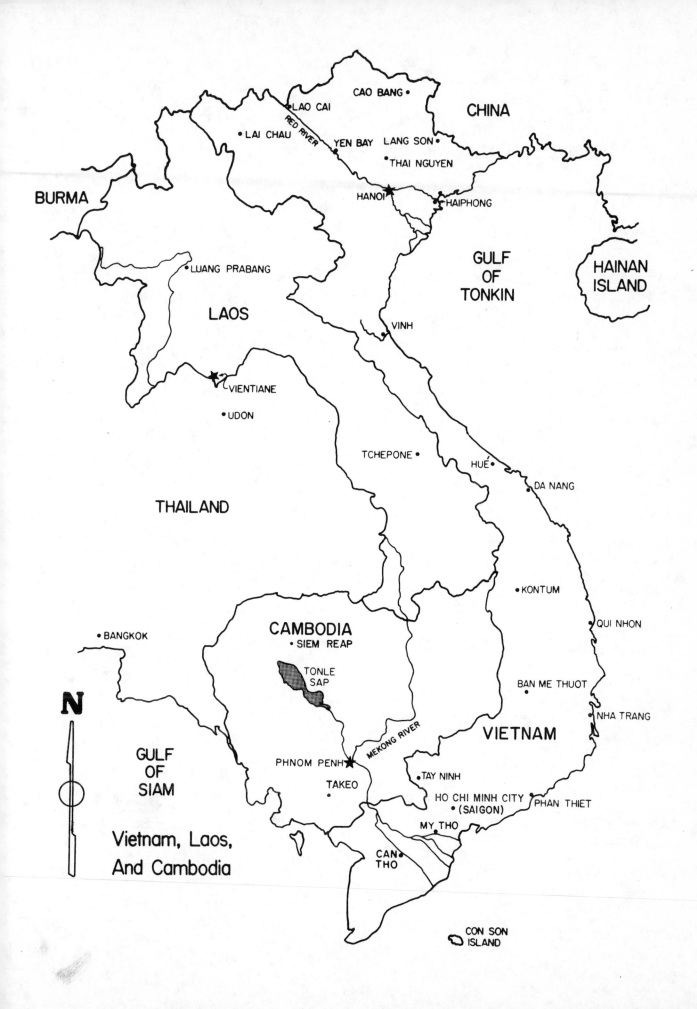

CHINA

CAO BANG •

• LAO CAI

• LAI CHAU

RED RIVER

YEN BAY

LANG SON •

• THAI NGUYEN

HANOI ★

• HAIPHONG

BURMA

• LUANG PRABANG

LAOS

GULF
OF
TONKIN

HAINAN
ISLAND

VIENTIANE ★

• UDON

VINH •

TCHEPONE •

HUÉ •

THAILAND

• DA NANG

• KONTUM

• BANGKOK

CAMBODIA

• SIEM REAP

TONLE
SAP

QUI NHON •

BAN ME THUOT •

NHA TRANG •

MEKONG RIVER

VIETNAM

N

PHNOM PENH ★

GULF
OF
SIAM

• TAKEO

• TAY NINH

HO CHI MINH CITY
• (SAIGON)

• PHAN THIET

Vietnam, Laos,
And Cambodia

MY THO •

CAN
THO •

CON SON
ISLAND

VIETNAM SINCE THE FALL OF SAIGON

VIETNAM SINCE THE FALL OF SAIGON

William J. Duiker

The Pennsylvania State University

Ohio University
Center for International Studies
Southeast Asia Series No. 56
1980

Library of Congress Cataloging in Publication Data

Duiker, William J   1932–
  Vietnam since the fall of Saigon.

  (Papers in international studies: Southeast Asia
series; no. 56)
  Bibliography: p.
  1. Vietnam—History—1975–   I. Title. II. Series.
DS559.912.D84   959.704′4   80-21166
ISBN 0-89680-106-3

Table of Contents

List of Maps

Dedicated

to

Ottilie,

who is all that a mother-in-law

should be, and more.

Acknowledgements

Because of the limited and scattered nature of documentary sources on the history of modern Vietnam, students of the Vietnamese revolution are compelled, perhaps more than most, to rely on their friends and colleagues for assistance in locating useful materials. Such is certainly the case here. I am indebted to Tony Mano, David Marr, Carl Thayer, and Pete Barnes for providing me with such materials at various times. Douglas Pike and Bill Turley have thoughtfully sent me copies of their own articles on the subject, and thus provided me with interesting insights. I am particularly grateful to King C. Chen for sending me his copies of the 1978 Black Paper issued by the Pol Pot regime, and the Vietnamese White Paper of 1979. The Information and Privacy Staff of the Department of State was helpful in locating materials in Central Foreign Policy Records that were used in the course of this study. I would like to extend my appreciation to the Institute for the Arts and Humanistic Studies, and the College Fund for Research of the College of Liberal Arts at The Pennsylvania State University for providing financial assistance. Finally, I would like to thank my mother, Jeanne S. Duiker, for providing me with a home away from home and a base of operations while in Washington, and my wife, Yvonne, for just being here.

William J. Duiker
The Pennsylvania State University

VIETNAM SINCE THE FALL OF SAIGON

Revolution does not conclude with the storming of the Bastille. Historical experience demonstrates that the seizure of power is only the first, and
not necessarily the most complex and difficult step in the revolutionary process. Power must be consolidated and the remaining forces of the opposition
eliminated. Tensions within the camp of the victors must be averted, or at
least minimized, lest the various elements in the radical alliance turn on
each other and lead the revolution into anarchy. A new revolutionary program
must be drafted to broaden the base of the support for the new order among the
masses. Finally, the population must be mobilized to prepare for the defense
of the revolution from its external enemies.

The communists, on coming to power in South Vietnam at the end of April
1975, were not unaware of such problems, and they were prepared to take measures to resolve them.   Indeed, it is one of the strengths of communist
parties that they know what to do with power once they have it in their grasp.
For the Vietnamese, the basic documents came from Lenin and from Mao Tse-tung.
Lenin had provided affirmation of the need for a Dictatorship of the Proletariat led by its vanguard element, the communist party, until the power of
the bourgeoisie had been totally smashed.[1] And he came to realize that when
the communists come to power in a backward society in which the capitalist
sector had not yet fully ripened, the revolutionaries must themselves perform
certain tasks normally completed during the capitalist stage of development
(the transformation from small-scale to large-scale production, destruction
of the feudal landholding system and the distribution of excess land to poor
peasants, and a proper toleration of "bourgeois specialists" in order to
utilize their technological capacities in the interests of building an advanced
economy).

But it was Mao Tse-tung who first successfully applied the doctrine of
Marx and Engels to an Asian society almost totally lacking the objective conditions for a transition to socialism. In On New Democracy, Mao drew on
Lenin for the assumption that in Asia the capitalist class lacked the capacity
to wage the bourgeois democratic revolution, and contended that the communist
party could undertake the task of leading society through the capitalist stage,
and thence on to socialism.[2] During the first "New Democratic" stage of the
revolution, the Party would nationalize only the major industries, banks and
utilities, while encouraging local capitalists to increase production. The
land of the feudal landowning class would be divided among the poor, but rich
peasants would be left alone to encourage them to increase grain production.
Nationalization of commerce and industry in the cities, and collectivization
in rural areas, would be postponed until the second proletarian socialist stage
of the revolution.

Mao's key innovation, perhaps, lay in the realm of politics. Instead of
a Dictatorship of the Proletariat, or of the proletariat in alliance with the
poor peasantry, he called for a "People's Democratic Dictatorship" composed

of the Leninist four-class alliance of workers, peasants, petty bourgeoisie and national bourgeoisie, which would carry society through to the stage of communism and the final withering away of the state. As the sole organization to possess an understanding of sacred doctrine, the Communist Party would naturally be the dominant force, but other parties representing the various progressive social classes in the revolutionary alliance would be allowed to participate in the political process as well.

For a time after its formation in February of 1930, the Indochinese Communist Party (ICP) accepted theoretical direction from Comintern headquarters in Moscow. Only in 1941 did the ICP begin seriously to absorb the revolutionary experience of its fraternal party in China. At the famous Pac Bo Plenum held in the mountains of North Vietnam in May, the Party adopted the Maoist model of a guerilla strategy based on the concept of building up the revolutionary forces in liberated base areas and then seizing the cities from the countryside.[3] It also appropriated the Chinese concept of a broad national front (the famous Vietminh Front) led by the Party but based on an alliance of all patriotic classes. At that time, however, the ICP did not explicitly adopt Mao's strategy of New Democracy for the period after the seizure of power. In all probability that apparent oversight actually reflected the Party's view of the current situation in Vietnam; the main requirement for the moment was to maximize support for the struggle against the French colonial regime. This could best be done by disguising the Party's leading role in the Vietminh Front. Formal adoption of Mao's concept of New Democracy would advertise the Party's dedication to orthodox Marxist-Leninist principles and indicate its intention to carry Vietnamese society on to communism, thus alienating the support of moderates in the conflict against the French.

The first formal announcement that the Party intended to adopt the New Democratic model came at the Second National Congress, held in early 1951, at a time when the Party (now renamed the Vietnamese Workers' Party, or VWP) had more openly acknowledged its indebtedness to the new communist government in China for the military assistance provided by the latter to the Vietnamese struggle for national liberation. The programmatic document was the Political Report delivered by the Party's General Secretary, Truong Chinh. Chinh announced that the Vietnamese revolution took the form of a people's national democratic revolution led by the working class and based on the worker-peasant alliance. It would consist of a two-stage process: a first bourgeois democratic and a second proletarian socialist stage. The bourgeois democratic revolution would take place under the leadership of the Party, which would then guide the revolution directly to the socialist stage without passing through a separate stage of capitalist development.[4]

Three years after the close of the Second Congress, the Geneva Agreement divided Vietnam at the Seventeenth Parallel and placed the Northern half of the country under communist rule. At a plenary session of the Central Committee held shortly after the conclusion of the Accords in July of 1954, it was decided that the North could move directly toward the construction of socialism before the final reunification of the two zones. In conformity with the New Democratic model, however, the Party leadership adopted a policy of gradualism in order to complete the tasks of the capitalist revolution before initiating

the advance toward socialism. Banks, utilities, and major commercial and manufacturing enterprises were seized by the government, but most small businesses
were permitted to remain under private ownership in order to encourage production. In rural areas, land reform was instituted, with over half of all peasant families in the North receiving land under the program. Only in 1958 did
the regime begin to move directly toward socialism with the institution of
collective farms in the countryside.

The results were mixed. From an ideological standpoint, the program was
a relative success. Within a few years the bulk of the rural economy had been
placed under collective ownership. State-owned enterprises gradually became
dominant in the manufacturing and commercial sector. From a purely economic
point of view, however, the Party was destined to be disappointed, for in the
task of increasing production and building the foundations of an advanced
socialist society, performance did not match expectations. Little progress
was achieved in transforming the economy from small-scale to large-scale production. Labor productivity remained low, and few of the regime's production
goals were met. Grain output lagged, and with a burgeoning population, the
ratio of man versus land in the countryside increased at an alarming rate.
Much of the problem, of course, could be attributed to the resumption of the
revolutionary struggle in the South during the early 1960s. For over a decade,
the Northern economy was geared primarily to provide rear support in the
struggle for reunification. Its industrial base was badly damaged by inten-
sive American bombing. Much of the working-age population was drafted into the
armed forces. At war's end, the North Vietnamese economy was badly in need of
attention.[5]

On the morning of April 30th, 1975, communist tanks rumbled down the leafy
avenues of downtown Saigon and up onto the spacious green lawn of the Presiden-
tial Palace. A North Vietnam soldier mounted the roof of the Palace, lowered
the red and yellow striped flag of the GVN (Government of Vietnam), and hoisted
the standard of the Provisional Revolutionary Government (PRG) in its place.
Two hours earlier, in a radio broadcast from the Palace, President Duong Van
Minh had called on all South Vietnamese forces to lay down their arms. Then
Minh and his cabinet awaited the inevitable and with the arrival of the first
communist units, surrendered meekly. After over a decade of bitter struggle,
the long conflict had ended, not with a bang, but with a whimper.

The original plans of the Party leadership for consolidation in the South
had been colored by the realities of the war. As in the early stages of the
conflict against the French over a decade earlier, one of the major objectives
was to disguise the leading role of the Party in the revolutionary struggle
against the Saigon regime in order to avoid alienating important sectors of
moderate opinion in the South. The program of the National Liberation Front
or NLF (the equivalent of the Vietminh Front of the 1940s) had deliberately
avoided references to Party rule after the victory of the revolution and had
talked in general terms of the formation of a "democratic government of
national union" composed of representatives from all progressive sectors of
South Vietnamese society. Politically, the NLF promised to ensure broad democratic freedoms. In the economic sphere, it made no mention of communism and
called simply for the confiscation of the property of the American imperialists

and their puppets. The right of private ownership of the means of production would be protected. In rural areas, a program of "land to the tiller" would be instituted, and the new government would "confirm and protect the peasants' ownership of lands allotted to them by the revolution." At some unspecified point in the future, the reunification of the two zones would be achieved on the basis of peaceful negotiations.[6]

The emphasis on gradualism reflected the Party's need to appeal to moderates in the struggle against the Saigon government. It also reflected its assumption that victory would probably not be realized through a direct military takeover of the South by the revolutionary forces, but as the result of a negotiated settlement resulting in the creation of a coalition government including both communist and non-communist elements. In the Party's plan, this transitional regime would gradually be replaced by a government under total Party control and the final reunification with the North.[7]

As it turned out, the final triumph was achieved by military means, and the Party did not have to share power. The decision to opt for a totally military solution appears to have been made early in 1975, in response to the unexpected weakness of the Saigon regime and the evident determination of the Ford Administration not to re-enter the conflict. During the final days of the war, high political figures in South Vietnam maneuvered frantically in an effort to arrange a negotiated settlement with Hanoi, or with the PRG, its surrogate in the South. To the last there were tantalizing rumors that even at that late date the communists might be willing to settle for a negotiated agreement. But the Party's long-time strategy of a transitional regime had now been overtaken by events. With total military victory at hand, Hanoi now decided to dispense with the stage of a coalition regime. Even after President Nguyen Van Thieu stepped down, ultimately to be replaced by General Duong Van Minh, long rumored to be an acceptable figure to the communists, it did not relent. Hanoi's response to Minh's final desperate appeal, in the form of a directive to the Southern military command, was terse and to the point:

> Continue the attack on Saigon according to plan, advancing
> in the most powerful spirit, liberate and take over the whole
> city, disarm enemy troops, dissolve the enemy administration
> at all levels, and thoroughly smash all enemy resistance.[8]

Consolidation

The first task of the new rulers in South Vietnam was to fill the vacuum left by the virtual disintegration of the previous regime. The rapidity of Saigon's collapse caught the Party leadership by surprise and during the final campaign, as the hammerblows of the PAVN (People's Army of Vietnam) were striking ever closer to the capital, a Military Management Committee was hurriedly set up, under the chairmanship of General Tran Van Tra, long-time commander of revolutionary forces in the South.

The obvious purpose of preceding civilian with military rule was to facilitate the restoration of order and the elimination of hostile remnants of the previous regime's armed forces. There were signs that this task would not be difficult. Most of the leading members of the old regime, including President Thieu, had already fled the country by ship, by plane, or in the American helicopters that had risen like gigantic birds over the sky of Saigon during the war's final hours. Of those government and military officials who remained, a few fled to the hills and the swamps to continue the struggle, but most accepted the inevitable and awaited their fate. As for the population as a whole, there were undoubtedly many who welcomed the results, but (if reports by foreign observers can be judged reliable) most appeared to accept the new masters less with enthusiasm or fear than with resignation. If this proved to be the case, the communists would have time to work their miracle.[9]

The new authorities immediately set to work to bring order out of chaos. The Military Management Committee under General Tran Van Tra began to set up a new revolutionary administration in the South and issue directives. At all levels, People's Revolutionary Committees were formed to provide a temporary administrative apparatus prior to the holding of elections. Local militia units under Party direction maintained revolutionary order and searched for recalcitrant elements loyal to the old regime. The Party's secret apparatus surfaced and dispatched revolutionary cadres to all city wards and subwards and to rural villages to register the local population and single out reactionaries for relocation and punishment. Where necessary, support was provided by North Vietnamese military units in the vicinity. Former military and civilian officials from the previous regime were ordered to report to the new revolutionary authorities. They were then classified into various categories. Those considered a threat to the new order were told to return home to await further instructions (most of these would later attend brief indoctrination sessions); others were directed to report to re-education camps, usually for a few weeks of political indoctrination. The worst offenders were sent to isolated work camps, where they were expected to remain for an extended period of time. Informed observers estimated that before the end of the year, several hundred thousand members of the previous government had been incarcerated in such centers.[10]

Beyond the immediate problem of restoring law and order in the South, the primary problem for the new regime would be to set the economic sector back on its feet. Saigon and many of the other major cities were a mess, while food production had been badly disrupted during the final military offensive. During the last years of the war thousands of peasants had fled from their native villages to escape the ravages of the war. According to a communist estimate, by the end of the conflict some 8 million Vietnamese, comprising 34% of the total population of the GVN, were living in the cities.[11] The flood of refugees from the villages added to an already serious problem of unemployment and **as it** seized power, the new communist government was faced with an estimate of more than three million persons unemployed in the city of Saigon alone.

The general policy of the Party leadership in the opening days was to move slowly and carefully in order to reassure the local population in the South and restore normal operations. Directives issued by the new authorities called on merchants to open their shops, who were reassured that their profits would be guaranteed by the new government. The regime did make an effort to round up undesirable elements - beggars and street urchins, bargirls and prostitutes - but to avoid panic, all signs of mass arrests or an incipient bloodbath were

avoided. In a few cases, revolutionary zealots ranged throughout downtown
Saigon attacking local youths in Western dress. In a few cases Southerners
were dragged from buses to have their long hair sheared and their Western-
style clothing ripped to shreds. Government directives soon appeared in the
press, however, warning that such revolutionary excesses would be severely
punished.

On the other hand, the new regime moved expeditiously to eliminate or at
least reduce the "poisonous weeds" of Western bourgeois culture and plant the
seeds of a new and beautiful socialist culture. Books reflecting Western
influence were removed from bookstores and libraries. The playing of the most
obnoxious forms of Western music was banned. According to one report, Saigon
radio stations, now under Party control, were only permitted to play Western
music for two hours each day, and the beat and lyrics were toned down. The
key vehicle for controlling behavior and transmitting cultural values, of
course, was education. For a brief period, the entire school system was shut
down, and teachers were given reindoctrination courses before being certified
to teach under the new regime. When the schools reopened students were issued
new textbooks hurriedly sent down from the North to replace the existing ones
which were now withdrawn from circulation. A new curriculum was instituted
and based on the three-level system in use in North Vietnam.[12]

The major immediate task within the economic sector was to reduce the level
of unemployment in the big cities and restore food production in the countryside.
Encouraging businessmen and farmers to restore normal operations was a partial
answer at best. While many of the unemployed were peasants who had fled from
their villages to escape the effects of the war, other thousands were urban
residents who had been employed in service occupations stemming from the long
American presence in the South. With the departure of their clients and the
cutting of the umbilical cord to the American economy, the source of their
livelihood had been eliminated.

For the new regime, the logical answer was to reverse the flow to the
cities and encourage the population to return to the countryside. The effects
of the exodus from rural areas were clearly evident. Entire villages had been
virtually abandoned and agricultural production had significantly declined.
According to one communist estimate, agricultural production in 1975 represented only about ten percent of the entire gross national product of South
Vietnam.[13] With the overcrowded North chronically short of food, the restoration of the rice-rich South to its historic role of breadbasket of Vietnam was
undoubtedly a matter of high priority to the Party leadership.

The primary means utilized to repopulate the countryside was the formation
of so-called New Economic Areas (NEAs). The concept had originated during the
First Five-Year Plan in the early 1960s when planners in the DRV had called for
the coordination and diversification of agriculture and industry through the
construction of middle-sized urban centers encompassing both food production
and manufacturing. Set up at the district level, these new population centers
(described as the "urbanization of the countryside") were to be located where
possible in underdeveloped areas in the mountains and plateau regions, thus
bringing virgin lands into cultivation, and providing new foci for industrial

development, or at least industrial self-sufficiency, in the countryside. The
plan was initiated in 1961 and although hampered by poor planning and the
reluctance of the peasants, by the end of the war had resulted in the transfer
of nearly one million peasants from the crowded Red River Delta to the mountains
or foothills, thus creating several hundred new agricultural cooperatives and
clearing over 100,000 hectares of virgin land.[14]

With the return of peace, the concept of the New Economic Areas was resus-
citated as a means of resolving the economic crisis in the South. Plans were
hurriedly drafted to set up NEAs in underpopulated provinces throughout South
Vietnam. While a few were located in the Mekong Delta or along the Central
coast, most were established in the sparsely settled Central Highlands or in
the piedmont regions along the Cambodian border, where the effects of war had
been particularly severe. Theoretically, the locations were to be selected on
the basis of their economic potential, but it is likely that political and
security factors were often involved. Once the areas had been given on-the-
spot preparation by teams of cadres, they were considered ready for settlement
and the government would recruit volunteers, who would be provided with seeds,
farm implements, building materials, and sufficient food for several months.[15]

Government sources indicated that the ultimate objective was to settle up
to two million people in the new settlements. According to regulations, re-
cruitment was supposed to be on a voluntary basis, but complaints soon appeared
in the press that certain categories of citizens - members of the previous
regime, the minorities, the poor and unemployable - were being forcibly recruited.
The problem was exacerbated when reports began to filter back from the new settlements of poor cadre preparation, lack of facilities, and economic hardship.
Nevertheless, by the end of the year the government announced that half a million Vietnamese had been transferred under the new program.

A second major problem for the new regime was to eliminate the influence
of private enterprise in the Southern economy and advance toward government
control over the means of production and distribution. So long as the bulk of
the manufacturing and commercial sector was under private control, the Party
would be unable to stabilize prices and the distribution of goods, and establish centralized planning procedures. Yet the process of undermining the
power of private capital must be undertaken in such a way as to minimize disruptive economic and political effects in the cities.

The first cautious moves by the new authorities were taken in the early
summer of 1975. All property owned by the GVN was confiscated, and private
banks and a number of enterprises belonging to foreign capitalists were seized. In
order to reduce the power of major industrialists and traders, the government
launched a campaign to confiscate the property of the so-called comprador
bourgeoisie (described in one article as bankers, war contractors, ex-imperial-
ists, investors and speculators). Contending that these elements were guilty
of speculation, hoarding, and related efforts to sabotage the efficient func-
tioning of the market, the government moved quickly to eliminate them by
seizing their businesses and confiscating their property in a campaign described
in the leading Saigon newspaper as "difficult, violent, and extremely complex."[16]

Several individual entrepreneurs, described as "the pharmaceutical king" or "the barbed wire king" were placed on trial and charged with serious crimes against the people. A few were executed after showtrials, presumably as a means to encourager les autres. The purpose of the campaign, according to the Party's theoretical journal Hoc Tap, was "to eliminate the traces of neo-colonialism, the comprador bourgeoisie, bureaucratic and militaristic remnants of the feudal system. ..." In order to prevent panic, the government used the time-tested united front approach and encouraged the Southern commercial middle class (in Marxist jargon, the national bourgeoisie, whose own "positive aspects" were to be encouraged) to "enthusiastically take part in the struggle" against reactionary elements.

A second measure to reduce the influence of private business in South Vietnam was the establishment of a new currency. The old piaster was abolished as a medium of exchange and replaced by a new Southern dong. The new currency was not to be interchangeable with the dong in use in the North, and was described as only temporary until final unification of the two zones. In theory all piasters held by private citizens in the South were to be exchanged for the new currency (at a rate of one dong for 500 piasters) but in reality each family possessing less than one million piasters was allowed to exchange up to 100,000 piasters (approximately U.S. $1,000) for 400 dong and deposit the remainder in the Central Bank.[17]

In rural areas, the new authorities moved with even greater caution. Although there were a few reports of class struggle in the countryside, there was no nationwide land reform campaign similar to that undertaken two decades earlier in the North, and the government announced that for the time being, land would remain in private hands. One official spokesman commented that there was no immediate need for land distribution since, for the most part, the power of the landlord class in the South had already been broken (a back-handed tribute to the "land to the tiller" program of the GVN in the late 1960s as well as a consequence of previous land reform campaigns in liberated areas).[18]

The primary immediate problem for the government was to attempt to stabilize the price of rice and guarantee an adequate supply for food for the urban population. To achieve these purposes new state stores were set up to purchase and market rice as a means of establishing control over price and distribution. Private retail merchants were permitted to remain in operation, but were now required to obtain a license from the local authorities. Individual farmers were pressed to make reciprocal contracts with government purchasing agents to provide a set amount of grain to the state. After fulfilling their tax obligation and turning in the rice required by their contracts, the farmers "must be allowed to freely trade their surplus rice on the market."[19]

For sensitive ears, there were signs that further changes were around the corner. Comments appeared in the press describing the formation of experimental cooperatives in rural areas. An article in Hoc Tap discussed a project to set up "large-scale state-operated farms" and "agricultural-industrial cooperatives" where conditions were appropriate, and spoke of the need to persuade farmers in a "gradual, positive and steady manner," of the value of cooperation.[20] As a first step in this direction, the government announced that work exchange teams (WETs) were to be formed where practicable. The WET, like its relatives the production solidarity team and the production collective, was a seasonal work-sharing arrangement among peasants that has been traditionally used by communist societies as the first stage in the socialization process.

In effect, the regime was taking the first tentative steps toward building socialism in the South while for the time being tolerating a significant degree of private enterprise in most sectors of the economy. This policy was illustrated by the announcement that for the foreseeable future the Vietnamese economy would be divided into five separate sectors: 1) state owned, 2) collective, 3) joint state-private enterprises, 4) private capitalism, and 5) individual ownership. Because of the strength of the socialist system in the North, observed one commentator, the presence of capitalist elements in the south could be temporarily tolerated.[21] This cautious approach undoubtedly reflected the Party's hope that economic progress could be achieved without unnecessarily disrupting the economy and arousing the hostility of the mass of the population.

If the first steps taken by the new regime showed a sense of caution and reflected the belief that at least for the time being, continued separation and the immediate needs of the population must take precedence over reunification and the revolution in production relations, by late summer signs began to appear which suggested that the Party leadership had begun to reevaluate its position. At the 24th plenary session of the Central Committee held in July and August at the mountain resort of Dalat in the Central Highlands, the Party decided to bypass a period of separate existence and New Democracy and move rapidly toward socialism and unification with the North. As the Resolution issued at the close of the Plenum pointed out, reunification would "create a new strength and new advantage for developing the economy and culture and consolidating National Defense."

Hints of these decisions began to appear in the press by late summer. Then, in early November, a conference of leading elements of the NLF, the Vietnamese Alliance of National Democratic and Peace Forces (a communist front similar to the NLF but designed especially to appeal to urban intellectuals), and the Advisory Council of the PRG (in the absence of an elected national assembly, this council temporarily played the role of the supreme legislative body in South Vietnam) was held in Saigon to discuss the issue of national reunification. Not surprisingly, the conference delegates formally approved the proposal for a rapid reunification of the two zones and an acceleration of the process of moving toward socialist forms of ownership in the South. Shortly after, representatives of the two zones met in a joint Political Consultative Conference to give the matter formal consideration.

The key decision was the one to abandon the earlier decision to nurse the South through a period of New Democracy prior to advancing to socialism. Truong Chinh, whose address was apparently viewed as the keynote speech of the conference, put it succinctly:

> South Vietnam has been carrying out a people's national demo-
> cratic revolution. At present, when it has been completely
> liberated, should South Vietnam limit itself within the people's

national democratic revolution for a period of time before
embarking on the socialist revolution to socialist construction? I think that is not necessary. The great victory of
the general offensive and uprising in the spring of this
year has put a victorious end to that phase of the people's
national and democratic revolution in South Vietnam and
opened up for the South Vietnamese people a new phase of
revolution with a new strategic task - that of socialist
revolution.[22]

In effect, Truong Chinh now called for the South to begin the process of transformation to socialism while at the same time completing the remaining tasks
of "New Democracy" - building a people's revolutionary administration, repres-
sing counter-revolutionaries, abolishing the feudal system of landownership
and establishing a program of "land to the tiller."

The decision to accelerate the pace of economic change was deliberately
linked to that of political reunification. As Truong Chinh put it, central
planning could not be successfully implemented until the country had first
been placed under a single administration. Unity must therefore first be
achieved at the governmental level, within the Party and in the mass organizations. Once political unification had been achieved, the South could "gradually transform the private capitalist industry and commerce, agriculture,
handicrafts and small trade along socialist lines, and set up the economic
sectors under the state, and collective management or under joint private-state
management."

Why did the Party decide to accelerate the process of economic and social
change in the South? In his address to the Political Consultative Conference,
Truong Chinh justified the move on the grounds that while there were a few
differences between the two zones, they were fundamentally similar in their
essential characteristics. The major differences, Chinh noted, were in the
economic structure (in the North collectives and the state-owned economy had
"absolute predominance," while in the South private ownership continued to be
the rule) and in the social class structure (in the North, the exploiters had
been essentially reformed, and there are only three classes - proletariat,
collective peasantry and socialist intellectuals - while in the South there
were peasants, workers, various types of bourgeoisie and the remnants of the
feudal class). Such differences, however, were only "conditional and temporary" while the similarities were "essential and decisive."

Comments in the official press which followed the close of the conference
amplified on Chinh's remarks. Several editorials pointed out that the situation in the South in 1975 differed in several major respects from that of the
North after the close of the Geneva Conference, when the New Democratic stage
remained in operation for several years. In the latter instance, the primitive
state of the Northern economy had compelled an extended period of economic
construction to raise the technical level of the economy prior to an advance
toward socialist production relations. By contrast, in 1975 the urban economy
in the South was relatively advanced (a grudging admission of one of the advantages of the capitalist system) and thus more capable of moving directly toward

socialist forms of ownership. In particular, the consumer industry was already well developed in South Vietnam and many towns and cities possessed a relatively advanced commercial and manufacturing sector. Moreover, the technological level of the population was high, and there was a large and dynamic petty bourgeoisie. Transportation and communications were quite sophisticated. Thus, conditions for rapid material and technological development were already present in the South.

A second favorable circumstance frequently mentioned was the fact that, unlike the North in 1954, where the remnants of the "feudal production system" were still in existence, the power of feudal landowners in rural areas of South Vietnam had already declined. Most of the cultivable land was already in the hands of private landowning peasants, and a comprehensive land reform program similar to that undertaken in the North in the mid-1950s would not be required as a preliminary step to collectivization.[23]

There may have been additional reasons for the decision. In the first place, resistance to the new regime may have collapsed more rapidly than had been anticipated. By late fall, armed opposition was limited to scattered groups operating in remote areas. More important, perhaps, by mid-summer the Party leadership had begun to appreciate the enormity of the task of restoring order in the economic sector, not only in the South but throughout the country as a whole, after a decade of war. The early moves to reassure the private economic sector had had only limited effect in raising production and reducing unemployment. The campaign against the comprador bourgeoisie had eliminated some of the more flagrant disruptive forces in the marketplace, but had not substantially reduced the problems of speculation and hoarding that created shortages and drove up consumer prices. Private farmers in the South were not selling their surplus grain to the state purchasing organizations but placing it on the private market or feeding it to their livestock. In effect, much of the Southern economy remained outside government control, and relatively immune to its influence. It is hardly surprising that Party leaders, convinced believers in the virtues of central planning, came to the conclusion that the nation's economic problems could only be resolved when the government had successfully removed what one commentator labelled the "harmful neo-colonalist garbage of the U.S. imperialists" and achieved firm control over the commercial and manufacturing sector in the South.

Another factor in the decision may have been the growing problems of coping with the "corrupt and parasitic" lifestyle of South Vietnamese society. Despite efforts to stamp out Western influence, it continued to exude its noxious fumes, and even threatened the revolutionary purity of Northern cadres and soldiers stationed in the South. Journals abounded with comments about drug addicts, decadent habits, and a hedonistic lifestyle. The authorities appeared to voice particular concern over evidence that it had begun to affect the attitudes of Party members and cadres. The latter were warned against corrupt habits, selfish individualism, laziness, and addiction to the pleasures of the decadent West. One report in a Hanoi publication even complained that soldiers returning from South Vietnam brought with them tape cassettes and then played (at high volume of course) Western rock music at all hours of the night, disturbing the repose of decent citizens.

Evidently not all Party members in the South were affected by the "temporarily shining" appearance of Western culture. Several reports in newspapers and journals noted that cadres and government officials in the South frequently did not understand the situation in South Vietnam, and failed to "respect the rights and freedoms of the masses." Some did not appear to realize that the transformation to socialism in the South "must be well prepared and carried out gradually and methodically." Others demonstrated an unreasonable suspicion of anyone of bourgeois extraction and did not realize that some individuals of reactionary class background could overcome their political weaknesses and transform themselves into useful and progressive members of society.[24] Clearly some cadres and officials in the South were being too enthusiastic in their efforts to create the socialist man.

Bureaucratic misbehavior in its diverse forms is no less common in communist societies than it is elsewhere. The problems that occurred in postwar South Vietnam could not be simply attributed to the lingering influence of Western culture, although that was undoubtedly a contributing factor. Indeed, reports of sluggishness, sickness, bureaucratism, "commandism," and rightism had permeated press reports about the bureaucracy in the North during the final years of the war. In 1974 the Politburo became sufficiently concerned to issue Resolution 228 which called for a campaign against "negative influences" in society and the economy. The end of the war, and the corrupt influences so prevalent in South Vietnamese society, inevitably exacerbated the problem. Reunification might be a way to alleviate the situation.

Although the decision to move rapidly to socialism reflected a high degree of official confidence in the industriousness, the talent, and the resilience of the Vietnamese people to recover rapidly from twenty years of armed conflict and launch immediately into an arduous and complex period of socialist construction, the leadership appeared aware of the enormity of the task ahead. Comments by official sources made it clear that the Party had a sober understanding of the process, and warned that it would require an extended period of time. One lengthy article which appeared in successive issues of the army newspaper Quan Doi Nhan Dan in the fall of 1975 acknowledged that "no matter how good we may be and no matter how great our efforts, we still need a period of many years, even tens of years, before all these difficulties are solved."[25] There was, then, a clear recognition that the road to socialism must be gradual, if direct. Another source quoted Lenin to the effect that no new class ever appeared on the stage of history to take power without undergoing a period of instability and violent shocks, of absurd turmoil, of confusion and useless activities."[26]

The completion of the process of reunification was achieved with relative ease. In December, the decision to move toward rapid reunification was given final ratification in both North and South - in the former by the National Assembly of the DRV, in the latter by a conference of people's representatives. In January, the South returned formally to civilian rule as the Military Management Committee handed over power to a fourteen member People's Liberation Committee under the chairmanship of Vo Van Kiet, formerly vice-chairman of the Saigon-Gia Dinh Military Management Committee. Then, in April, elections were held for a new National Assembly composed of representatives of both

zones. The new unified Assembly, slightly over half of whose members represented the North, approved the formation of a new unified Socialist Republic
of Vietnam (SRV), formally promulgated in July, and adopted a resolution to
draft a new constitution to take the entire country to socialism.[27]

The Five-Year Plan for 1976-1980

As Truong Chinh's speech at the Political Consultative Conference had made
clear, one of the most important consequences of reunification would be to permit the regime to integrate the Southern economy into the central planning
structure of the DRV. This, in turn, allowed the revival of the Second Five-
Year Plan, scheduled to begin operation in 1976. The Second Plan had been
drawn up soon after the 1973 Paris Agreement which had ended American involvement and put a temporary end to the war. A previous Plan had run from 1961 to
1965. A second had been scheduled to begin in 1966 but had been abandoned with
the escalation of the revolutionary struggle in the South and replaced with
annual plans, easier to coordinate with the war effort and more modest in their
objectives. In the immediate aftermath of the takeover of the South in 1975,
some thought was apparently given to scrapping the new Plan altogether until
the South had completed the stage of New Democracy. Eventually, however, Party
leaders decided to retain the Plan and include South Vietnam in their calcula-
tions. That decision was probably reached at the 24th Plenum of the Central
Committee in the summer of 1975, and was undoubtedly a major factor in the
decision to proceed directly toward the unification of the two regions into a
single economic and political unit.

Broadly speaking, the objectives of the new Five-Year Plan reflected the
three major goals which had characterized communist economic planning in Vietnam since the Third Party Congress in 1960, and had been designed to achieve
the transformation of Vietnamese society in terms of three revolutions in
1) production relations, 2) ideology and culture, and 3) science and technol-
ogy.[28] It is a measure of the essential pragmatism of the Party leadership
that of the three, the scientific and technological revolution was viewed as
the key factor. Indeed, although the spiritual revolution has been given
serious attention in Vietnam, the Party has always appeared to view the transformation from small-scale to large-scale production as the key component in
the struggle to build a socialist society. The magnitude of the task was
suggested in a report written by Le Duan earlier in the decade. Over 80
percent of all workers in the North were involved in manual labor. In the
collectives, only 6.5 percent of the entire cultivated area was plowed by
tractor. The DRV suffered from a serious shortage of trained technicians,
and managerial experience was weak. As Le Duan himself conceded, the Vietnamese communist movement was mature in people's war and waging the national
democratic revolution, but woefully weak in grasping the basic laws of
socialist construction.[29] A major goal of the Plan would thus be to promote
the transformation of the economic sector from small-scale to large-scale
production and thereby advance a significant step toward the creation of a
technologically-advanced socialist society. This objective could not be
realized within the scope of a single Five-Year Plan, of course, and was set
up as an ultimate goal to be achieved over a period of about thirty years.

In terms of specific goals, the new Plan placed predictably heavy emphasis on industrial development, and on improving the basic economic infrastructure in terms of energy output, transportation and communications, and coal mining. At the same time, the Plan's goals in the field of agriculture were also ambitious, calling for an annual growth rate of 7.8 percent in food production through water conservancy, increasing mechanization, double-cropping and the development of subsidiary crops. Heavy concentration would be placed on the building of agricultural-industrial units at the district level and on the movement of people from heavily populated provinces in the Red River Delta and along the Central coast to the underdeveloped areas. An article by Party planner Che Viet Tan in the February 1977 issue of the theoretical journal Tap Chi Cong San (the new name for Hoc Tap) indicated the extent of the Party's vision.[30] According to Tan, at the end of the war in 1975, 60 percent of the entire population of North Vietnam was concentrated in the Red River Delta and on the plains of Thanh Hoa and Nghe Tinh provinces. Despite the movement of one million people to New Economic Areas over the previous two decades, the population density per square kilometer in the Delta had risen from 488 in 1955 to 868 in 1975. The per capita cultivated area had declined from 1,190 square meters in 1955 to only 670 two decades later. With the population expected to nearly double over the next 25 years, Vietnam would have a population of about 100 million at the end of the century.

The regime's answer was to move nearly ten million people, mostly from the Red River Delta and the coastal lowlands, to new locations in the Central Highlands, the mountains in the North, the relatively unpopulated Mekong Delta, or to the offshore islands. This process would open up five million hectares of new land in the South, and relieve the congestion in the North. It would also provide the impetus for the creation of agricultural-industrial centers in the 500 districts around the country. According to plan, these new centers would serve to help consolidate the thousands of small population centers in rural areas into larger and more efficient ones consisting of 30,000 to 40,000 people. The entire process, according to Tan, would require at least twenty years. The goal of the current Plan would be to redistribute four million people, mostly through the establishment of NEAs.

One of the problems involved in the program was the effect it would have on Vietnamese relations with the tribal minorities. According to Tan's article, over the next two decades, over one and one-half million mountain tribesmen would be resettled and persuaded to abandon their nomadic way of life. In the meantime, other millions of ethnic Vietnamese would settle in areas previously reserved for minority use. The possible effect of such population movement on minority attitudes was enormous. Party policy must thus deal with the issue with the utmost circumspection. On the one hand, it must "ensure the political rights of all the ethnic minorities" and, on the other, "create conditions to eliminate, in a gradual and planned way, the differences concerning standards between the ethnic minority and the ethnic majority."[31] It would not be an easy task.

The second objective of the Plan was to "basically achieve" the socialist transformation of the Southern economy by 1980. This, too, would be difficult because of the entrenched capitalist habits of the local population. The program would be especially hampered by the fact that mechanization in the countryside was still limited. It would thus be necessary to persuade the peasant to accept collectivization prior to mechanization, to give up his land without the immediate promise of increased grain output and a higher standard of living. The process had succeeded in China where the peasant, in the immortal words of Mao Tse-tung, was "poor and blank." Could it succeed in South Vietnam, where capitalist practices held sway, even in rural areas? The regime's answer was to attempt to minimize the problem by increasing the availability of consumer goods at affordable prices (through increasing control over the manufacturing and commercial sector) and by combining collectivization with improved irrigation techniques and other measures to increase productivity. Based on the past record of the DRV, the prognosis could not be optimistic.

The final revolution, in the field of ideology and culture, would concentrate on eliminating the "noxious weeds" of Western bourgeois culture in the South and advance toward the creation of the "socialist man." But it would also require an improvement in attitudes and behavioral patterns among the population in the North. As Minister of Culture Hoang Minh Giam conceded, the Marxist-Leninist viewpoint had not yet "fully permeated the style of life" of the nation. "Feudal attitudes," a general term referring to a variety of social evils such as arrogance and "mandarinism," nepotism, sycophancy and the practice of backward family rituals, were still common among the population. And of course the most egregious symbol of the survival of capitalist attitudes in the countryside - the private plot - still survived in the collectives, and provided an estimated fifteen to twenty percent of total food production. There was no indication in the Plan that the regime intended to do away with the plots in the foreseeable future.

The problem would be particularly difficult in the South, of course, not least because of the presence of a number of religious groups like the sects and the Catholics traditionally hostile to Marxist ideology and practice. In particular, the Catholics appeared to excite the regime's concern. According to one government spokesman, although the Church hierarchy officially supported the new order, in actuality it was hostile, and he warned that the Church "must divest itself of imperialist influence." On the other hand, he noted that there was a gradual movement toward support of the revolution among the rank and file.[32] Similar problems were being encountered with the sects.

The central task of the Five-Year Plan in the area of ideology and culture was to attempt to replace the influence of Western culture and capitalist attitudes with a new socialist culture and lifestyle. In the words of Le Duan in his Political Report at the Fourth Party Congress:

> Our socialist literature and art should endeavor to create
> beautiful and varied artistic types concerning our new
> society and man, about the working class, collective peasantry,
> socialist intellectuals, officers and men of the people's army
> who reflect our people's revolutionary patriotism and other
> noble qualities. It must firmly assert the new system, the
> new way of life, the new morality and develop the fine national
> traditions and revolutionary traditions of our people.[33]

One of the prospective weaknesses of the Plan was inadequate financing. Vietnam was a poor country with meager reserves of foreign currency and an adverse balance of payments. Substantial amounts of foreign aid would be an absolute necessity if the Plan's goals were to be achieved. During the war, of course, Hanoi had received substantial assistance not only from the Soviet Union and China, but in smaller amounts from a number of Moscow's Eastern European allies. With the war at an end, however, a continuation of aid at high levels seemed doubtful. In late 1975 an agreement was reached with the Soviet Union calling for Soviet support in the construction of forty industrial projects, including the construction of a hydroelectric powerplant on the Black River. Additional assistance would be provided for the development of coal mining and oil prospecting. To remedy the serious lack of technological expertise in postwar Vietnam, several thousand students would be sent for training in the Soviet Union and other Eastern European countries.

Peking was evidently less generous. In talks held in Peking during the fall of 1975, Chinese negotiators appeared reluctant to increase their level of assistance to Vietnam and pointed out that, with the war over, Hanoi must learn how to apply the famous Maoist dictum of self-sufficiency.[34] An agreement was eventually reached, but it was limited to the maintenance of Chinese assistance at previous levels.

There were a number of other possible external sources for financial assistance, and several indicated an initial willingness to help build the new Vietnam. Hanoi was successful in negotiating aid and trade agreements with several countries outside the socialist camp, including Japan, France, and Sweden. Of particular importance were agreements with several Western European companies to explore for oil in the South China Sea. A new liberal investment code was promulgated in an effort to attract private foreign capital.

One of the major potential sources for aid outside the socialist countries, of course, was the United States. Here, however, it would be necessary to overcome the legacy of a generation of bitterness and mistrust. In the beginning, there were a few promising signs of a possible diplomatic breakthrough, leading to a normalization of relations between the former enemies. The Carter Administration which came into office in January of 1977 appeared receptive to negotiations leading to the establishment of normal diplomatic and commercial ties and voiced a willingness to consider such moves without preconditions. Clearly the new Administration wished to avoid a repetition of the long period of mutual hostility that had marked relations between Washington and Peking after the Civil War in China.

Here, however, Hanoi miscalculated. At the time of the conclusion of the Paris Agreement of 1973, President Nixon had allegedly committed the United States to provide U.S. $3.2 billion in postwar reconstruction assistance to the two Vietnams. Now Hanoi insisted that such aid be provided as a condition of diplomatic recognition and commercial relations. Talks held between Vietnamese and American representatives in Paris were friendly, but the latter made it clear that it would be virtually impossible to push any form of reconstruction aid to Vietnam through Congress. President Carter tried to surmount the problem by promising that the United States would "respond well" on the issue of possible economic assistance to Vietnam, but stated categorically that any such aid could not be considered as a form of war reparations. The problem was not resolved, however, and the two sides agreed to adjourn the talks and resume them at a later date.

The Fourth Party Congress

Within a little over a year, the communist regime had made a number of basic decisions which would inevitably have momentous consequences for the future of Vietnamese society. In December of 1976, these decisions were submitted to the Party as a whole when the Fourth National Congress of the Vietnamese Workers' Party was convened in Hanoi. The VWP had not held a National Congress since September of 1960, when the Third Congress had approved the decision to launch revolutionary war in the South. Now, for the first time in a century, Vietnam was again under unified rule, and preparing to begin the advance to socialism. The Congress put the finishing touches on the creation of a new unified party (including both the VWP and its southern branch, the People's Revolutionary Party), to be called the Vietnamese Communist Party (VCP), representing over one million members in the South and North. Slightly over a third were reportedly Southerners. It elected an enlarged Central Committee of 133 members, and a Politburo of seventeen (with three alternates).

Not surprisingly, the Congress also ratified the new Five-Year Plan and the decision to advance to socialism. Yet there were signs that some were uneasy at the rapidity of the planned advance. In his Political Report to the Congress Party First Secretary Le Duan remarked that:

> we have not clearly understood the close relationship between the transformation of production relations and the development of productive forces in the condition of taking small production to large-scale socialist production.

Moreover, at the Congress, several top members, including Hoang Van Hoan, founding member of the ICP, Politburo members since 1956, ex-Ambassador to China and currently vice-chairman of the Standing Committee of the National Assembly, lost their positions in the Party. While the precise reasons for the purge are still not clear (it was speculated at the time than Hoan had stepped down because of age), it later became clear that there was a moderate faction in the Party leadership which opposed the Heaven-storming approach taken by the majority. If the Party as a whole was moving resolutely into the future, there were doubters.[35]

Revolution and Foreign Policy

If the ambitious social and economic goals of the new SRV were to be successfully realized, certainly one of the major prerequisites would be a period of tranquility in Vietnamese foreign relations. Peace would permit a reduction in the military budget and in the size of the regular armed forces, now numbering over 600,000. Additional units of the PAVN could be assigned

duties in national construction, such as the clearing of virgin lands, the building of NEAs, and various water and flood control projects. Scarce national
resources could be channeled into useful construction projects, and into
improving the educational system, badly strained by years of war and conscription.

A similar situation had arisen in 1954 after the Geneva Agreement and the
communist occupation of North Vietnam. At that time, for a variety of reasons,
the Party had adopted a cautious foreign policy, concentrating on domestic
concerns while attempting to avoid a reopening of the military struggle in the
South. Only in 1959, when the visible decline of the Ngo Dinh Diem regime
had made prospects for victory there appear increasingly bright, had the
Party leadership adopted a new policy calling for a return to revolutionary
war. There were equally persuasive reasons for stressing internal needs over
an adventurous foreign policy after the fall of Saigon in 1975. Yet there
were also a number of strong crosscurrents impelling the SRV to maintain an
active and even aggressive foreign policy. In part, this can be ascribed to
the centrifugal force produced by all great social revolutions, a messianistic
urge to carry The Word to neighboring peoples, and an enduring suspicion
(sometimes justified) of hostile forces lurking abroad and awaiting an opportunity to undo the work of the revolution. Among other examples, both the
Soviet Union and the People's Republic of China had passed through a brief
period of revolutionary universalism after the completion of their own triumph
over reactionary internal forces.[36]

The Vietnamese were not immune to this familiar revolutionary pattern.
Following the seizure of Saigon, Party leaders appeared to experience a brief
period of hubris (certainly justified, under the circumstances), and a spate
of articles appeared in the press declaring that the victory of the Vietnamese
struggle for national liberation marked the opening of a new era in the history
of the world revolution, and the final stage of decline for world imperialism
led by the United States. Several commentaries noted that the conflict reflected
the convergence of three great revolutionary currents in the modern world -
of national independence, of democracy, and of socialism. Put in practical
terms, this meant that the Vietnamese revolution had demonstrated that a national
liberation struggle led by a Marxist-Leninist party could come to power in a
former colonial society, even against the concerted opposition of an imperialist
superpower like the United States.[37]

It is perhaps worthy of note that the Party leadership publicly declared
a sense of responsibility to promote successful revolutionary struggles
throughout the Third World. For example, in a speech on the basic principles
of Vietnamese foreign policy given before the new united National Assembly in
June of 1976, Le Duan noted that the basic principles of Vietnamese foreign
policy consisted of the following: 1) to endeavor to consolidate and strengthen
the militant solidarity and relations of socialist cooperation with socialist
countries and to contribute to restoring solidarity on the basis of Marxism-
Leninism and Proletarian Internationalism, 2) to safeguard and develop relations with Cambodia and Laos, 3) to fully support the just struggle of the
peoples of Southeast Asia for national independence, democracy and social
progress, and to achieve true independence and neutrality without the presence

of imperialist military bases and armed forces, 4) to fully support the just struggle of the Asian, African and Latin American countries against imperialism and colonialism, 5) to fully support the just cause of the workers in capitalist countries, 6) to establish normal relations with countries possessing different social systems on the basis of respect for independence, sovereignty, equality and mutual benefit, and 7) to continue the joint struggle against the policy of aggression and war led by the United States.[38]

While the language of Hanoi's call to revolutionary struggle had strong ideological overtones, under the surface there were more primordial factors at work intensifying the temptation to promote the revolution beyond its own borders. By definition, all national revolutions have among their primary objectives the enhancement of the security of the nation, and the realization of national unity within its natural historical and cultural frontiers. By the same token, they frequently release traditional ambitions for territorial expansion, and to realize the historic "national destiny" of the race. The French Revolution of 1789, and its counterparts in Russia and China in the modern era, all unleashed forces combining revolutionary messianism with a fervent and aggressive patriotism.

Vietnam could hardly avoid similar pressures. In the precolonial era it was the most dynamic society on the Southeast Asian mainland. After restoring its independence from China in the tenth century the Vietnamese empire had spread south from the Red River Valley along the coast, absorbing the state of Champa and seizing the lower Mekong Delta from the declining Angkor Empire (the predecessor of Cambodia) along the way. Then it began to expand westward and competed with the Kingdom of Siam over domination of Laos and Cambodia. The French conquest at the end of the nineteenth century temporarily interrupted the process and established clearly demarcated territorial boundaries to preserve the sanctity of Cambodia and Laos through the creation of separate protectorates. With the departure of the French, however, the historic Vietnamese urge to expand to the South and West now appeared to reassert itself. The Saigon regime refused to accept the borders established between Cambodia and Vietnam by the French (nor, in fairness, did Phnom Penh accept Vietnamese control over the lower Mekong Delta). For a time, the communists appeared to be immune from the temptation of national expansionism. In the mid-1960's Hanoi and its surrogate in the South, the National Liberation Front, reached agreements with the Sihanouk government in Phnom Penh which appeared to grant explicit recognition of the sovereignty and territorial integrity of Cambodia. To be sure, there were signs that Hanoi harbored aspirations of its own to establish a dominant position throughout the entire region of Indochina. The most prominent, and certainly the one most often cited, was the reference in the programmatic documents of the Indochinese Communist Party to the eventual formation of an Indochinese Federation comprising the three nations of the French-controlled Indochinese Union – Vietnam, Laos, and Cambodia.

In recent years, Hanoi has denied its intention to compel the new communist states of Cambodia and Laos to form a tripartite Indochinese Federation under Vietnamese domination, and points out that the reference to such a federation was formally abandoned at the Party's Second National Congress in 1951. It is also worthy of mention that the reference to "Indochina" in the program and title of the ICP in 1930 reflected not so much the views of the founding members of the Party as of Comintern headquarters in Moscow. At a meeting held in South China in February 1930 under the chairmanship of Ho Chi Minh, Party leaders had selected the name Vietnamese Communist Party (Viet Nam Cong San Dang). It was the current belief in Moscow, however, that small colonial countries like Vietnam, Laos, and Cambodia would be unable to achieve national liberation on their own. Comintern headquarters therefore directed the Vietnamese revolutionaries to take the name of Indochinese Communist Party (Dang Cong San Dong Duong), a shift in nomenclature which was approved, apparently with some reluctance, at the first meeting of the Party's Central Committee held in October. One reason for that reluctance was that during the prewar period, there were few if any native Laotians or Cambodians within the Party. The only Party cells formed in those two protectorates consisted of native Vietnamese.[39]

In 1951 the Second Congress of the Party, now renamed the Vietnam Workers' Party (VWP), withdrew references to the ultimate formation of an Indochinese Federation. At that time separate communist movements, the Laotian People's Revolutionary Party (LPRP), and the Pracheachon or People's Revolutionary Party were founded in Laos and Cambodia respectively. In March, a conference attended by representatives of the three revolutionary organizations approved the formation of an alliance based on "free choice, equality, and mutual assistance."[40]

It is worth noting, however, that even after the formation of separate communist movements in Laos and Cambodia, these organizations continued to receive direction from the VWP which, in the words of an internal document, still reserved "the right to supervise the activities of its brother parties in Cambodia and Laos." A special bureau was established under the VWP Central Committee to handle Cambodian and Laotian affairs. Moreover, despite Hanoi's later protestations to the contrary, the Vietnamese evidently did not totally abandon the vision of a federation. In the words of one internal Party document written at the time:

> Each nation – Vietnam, Cambodia, and Laos, has its own Party . . . Later, however, if conditions permit, the three revolutionary Parties of Vietnam, Cambodia, and Laos will be able to unite to form a single Party: the Party of the Vietnam-Khmer-Laotian Federation.[41]

Why, then, was it necessary to establish three separate parties, since militarily the entire region of Indochina at that time consisted of a single combat zone? According to the document cited above, there were two basic reasons: 1) the Laotian and Cambodian revolutions were at a different stage than the one in Vietnam (while the goal in the latter was to move rapidly towards socialism, the immediate objective of the revolutions in Laos and Cambodia was to set up a "popular democracy"), and 2) retention of the name "Indochinese" would:

> probably have prejudiced the support given by the Vietnamese revolution to the revolutions in Laos and Cambodia. The nationalist elements of Laos and Cambodia might have suspected

Vietnam of wishing to control Cambodia and Laos. The band of imperialists and puppets would have been able to launch coun- ter-propaganda destined to separate Vietnam from Cambodia and Laos, fomenting trouble among the Cambodian and Laotian peoples. Such an atmosphere of distrust could have harmed the unity of these nations in their fight against the French.

Since 1951, the Vietnamese Party leadership has carefully refrained from statements that might inflame patriotic sentiments among the fraternal Laotian and Cambodian peoples. But it was clear that Hanoi continued to view rela- tions with Cambodia and Laos as a keystone in Vietnamese foreign policy, not only during the war in the South but afterward as well. In his speech on foreign policy cited above, Le Duan mentioned the importance of friendly relations with its immediate neighbors as a crucial element in Vietnamese foreign policy.

If the desire for an intimate relationship with Laos and Cambodia was one of the pillars of Vietnamese foreign policy, another unquestionably was alliance with the Soviet Union. The Party's close relationship with Moscow dated back to even before its founding in 1930. Several of the early leaders of the ICP, including Ho Chi Minh, received their ideological training in Moscow, and during its first decade of existence the Party accepted strategi- cal guidance from the Comintern. The only open gesture of independence from Moscow came from a small but vociferous Trotskyite faction composed primarily of Paris-trained intellectuals based in Saigon. After 1941 the ICP adopted an independent strategy more in keeping with conditions in Vietnam, but it still made reliance on the Soviet Union the kingpin of its foreign policy. This relationship was based partly, but not entirely, on diplomatic and military dependence. Actually, the level of Soviet material assistance to the Vietminh movement in its struggle against the French was severely limited. At that time, the Vietnamese appeared to view the Soviet Union in a more abstract sense, as ideological mentor and their link with the outside world. During the later war against the Americans, of course, Soviet military and economic aid was crucial to communist success. By then, however, Hanoi had begun to demonstrate an increasing degree of independence from Moscow, and when the Khrushchev leadership attempted to dissuade the VWP from provoking an open confrontation with the United States in the early 1960s, Hanoi's foreign policy shifted temporarily towards Peking. The Brezhnev regime which rose to power in 1964 was more sympathetic to the Party's struggle in the South and granted sufficient aid to permit Hanoi to match the American military escalation. While Moscow and Hanoi did not agree on all issues, both found the relationship useful. For the Vietnamese it had become the kingpin of their foreign policy.

The relationship with China was more ambiguous. Prior to the Second World War the ICP had maintained tenuous contacts with the Chinese Communist Party (CCP), but the relationship lacked the warmth and intimacy of the Party's ties with the CPSU. With the victory of the CCP in the Civil War in 1949, the Vietnamese turned to China for military aid as well as strategical and ideo- logical guidance. It was at that point, for the first time, that the Party leadership publicly announced that the Vietnamese struggle for national libera- tion was based on the Chinese model.

If recent charges from Hanoi can be believed, however, it did not take long for the Vietnamese to begin to develop suspicions of Chinese intentions. According to the recent statement on Sino-Vietnamese relations published by the SRV Ministry of Foreign Affairs in late 1979, at the 1954 Geneva Conference Chou En-lai compelled the Vietnamese to conclude a compromise peace with France. He also deliberately attempted to divide the VWP from its allied parties in Laos and Cambodia in an effort to increase Chinese influence in Indochina.[42]

Whatever the truth of these charges, they did not lead at the time to a serious break in relations. During the immediate post-Geneva period, Hanoi's ties with Peking may have been cool, but they were correct, and with the outbreak of the Sino-Soviet dispute in the early 1960s, Hanoi attempted to maintain relatively good relations with both communist powers. The Party was not averse to manipulating the situation to its own advantage, but it was basic policy to avoid choosing sides in the dispute. After 1964, however, that balancing act became increasingly difficult to maintain. According to the Vietnamese, in that year Peking offered a program of massive assistance to the DRV on condition that the latter reject aid from Moscow. Although at that time Hanoi's relations with Moscow were strained the offer was refused, and before the year was out the DRV had received a commitment for increased assistance from the new Brezhnev leadership that succeeded to power in the Soviet Union.

Throughout the remainder of the war China continued to supply a substantial amount of material assistance to Vietnam. But the DRV, although carefully avoiding an openly pro-Soviet stance in the ideological dispute with China, refused Chinese advice and persistently rejected Peking's efforts to detach Hanoi from its growing reliance on Soviet Union. In turn, the Vietnamese were irritated by China's decision to seek a rapproachement with the United States in the early 1970s, a move which they feared would undermine Chinese support for the struggle in South Vietnam. In particular, Hanoi was angry at the timing of President Nixon's visit to Peking in 1972, at a moment when the Vietnamese were preparing to launch a major offensive against the Saigon regime.[43]

At war's end, then, Hanoi's traditional policy of maintaining friendly relations with both Moscow and Peking had begun to fray at the edges. The shift toward the Soviet Union was illustrated during the trade talks held with both Moscow and Peking in the fall of 1975. The talks with China did not go well. While the PRC refused to grant the full amount of aid requested by Hanoi, the Vietnamese rejected China's analysis of the global situation and Le Duan's departure from Peking was not marked by the usual joint communique. By contrast, Duan's visit to Moscow a month later was marked by apparent cordiality. The aid agreement may not have met with all of Hanoi's expectations, but it was substantial. In return, Le Duan voiced near total support for Soviet foreign policy.

The end of the war thus appears to have marked a significant shift in Vietnamese foreign policy away from nonalignment in the Sino-Soviet dispute and towards a clear preference for Moscow. Some observers have seen pragmatic

considerations at the root of this decision. The Soviet Union was obviously in
a better position than the PRC to provide Vietnam with the massive economic assistance required for postwar construction. The Party leadership may well have decided that a policy of "lean to one side" was justified if it served to persuade
Moscow to finance Hanoi's ambitious plans for socialist reconstruction. Yet there
were probably deeper underlying issues at work as well. One of the more notable
features in the 1979 statement is the high degree of Vietnamese suspicion and
hostility for China's long-range intentions in Southeast Asia. Territorial
disagreements, carefully hidden during the war, were beginning to emerge into
open view. Beneath it all lay a primordial distrust of China which transcended
the ties of ideology and practical interest and must have festered under the
surface during a generation of outward intimacy. It is not necessary to believe
that the Vietnamese party leadership was united on this issue. Rumors during
the Vietnam war of the existence of pro-Peking and pro-Moscow factions within the
Central Committee have never been confirmed, and if they existed, were kept in
check by Ho Chi Minh's delicate balancing act and the exigencies of the war.
With Ho's death in 1969 and the fall of Saigon six years later the factors
inhibiting increased hostility between Vietnam and China had been significantly
weakened. This issue may have come to a head at the Fourth Party Congress and
led to the purge of Hoang Van Hoan and several of his pro-Chinese associates.
It need not be maintained that Hanoi deliberately chose to provoke Peking by
siding with Moscow (after all, an open conflict with China could hardly be in the
Vietnamese interest). It is not improbable, however, that Hanoi saw the risk and
was willing to take it.[44]

Tension with Cambodia

Given the magnitude of Hanoi's domestic problems, it seems likely that
the Party leadership hoped to avoid foreign policy difficulties during the
months following the takeover in the South. Statements in the official
press indicated a general and continuing concern for national defense, and the
Resolution issued at the 24th Plenum held in July had called for measures to
defend the revolution against "imperialist plots." To deal with such changes,
the Central Committee directed the Ministry of Education to put national
defense issues and military training into the academic curriculum. But there
was a limited demobilization of the armed forces, and a number of units kept
on active duty were assigned to tasks of national construction.

It seems doubtful, then, that the tension which erupted between Vietnam and
the new revolutionary government of Democratic Kampuchea was of Hanoi's doing.
That tension, it is now clear, had been building up for years. Cambodia had
received its formal independence in 1953 as a consequence of the Geneva Accords.
During the 1950s the young Cambodian revolutionary movement, the Pracheachon, had
little success under the relatively benign and popular rule of Prince Norodom
Sihanouk. This apparently accorded with the interests of Hanoi at the time, which
considered the relatively neutralist stance of Sihanouk's government useful to
the revolutionary cause in Vietnam. Until the mid-1960s, the Vietnamese were
able to dissuade the leaders of the Cambodian revolutionary movement from
adopting a policy of active resistance to the government in Phnom Penh. Only
in September, 1960 was a Khmer Communist Party (KCP) founded and it, according to anti-Vietnamese sources in the movement, was a party in name only.
Throughout this period, there was disagreement with-

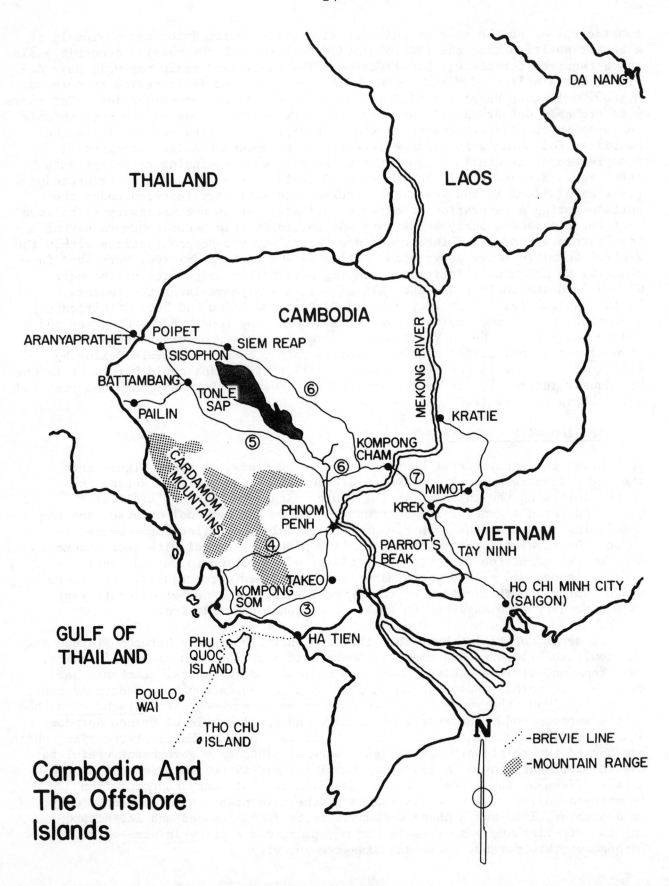

DA NANG

THAILAND

LAOS

CAMBODIA

MEKONG RIVER

ARANYAPRATHET
POIPET
SIEM REAP
SISOPHON
BATTAMBANG
TONLE SAP
PAILIN
⑥
KRATIE
⑤
KOMPONG CHAM
⑥
MIMOT
⑦
PHNOM PENH
KREK
CARDAMOM MOUNTAINS
VIETNAM
PARROT'S BEAK
TAY NINH
④
TAKEO
KOMPONG SOM
HO CHI MINH CITY (SAIGON)
③
GULF OF THAILAND
PHU QUOC ISLAND
HA TIEN
POULO WAI
THO CHU ISLAND

N

–BREVIE LINE
▒–MOUNTAIN RANGE

Cambodia And The Offshore Islands

in the young KCP over relations with Hanoi. Many of the early leaders were considered pro-Vietnamese, and several thousand had reportedly gone into exile in the DRV after the Geneva Conference. There was a radical faction within the Party, however, led by the Paris-trained intellectual Pol Pot (real name Saloth Sar), which opposed the Hanoi connection and distrusted Vietnamese intentions in Indochina.

In 1963 the Pol Pot faction seized power from its rivals in the Party. Under the new leadership the KCP was not only less inclined to accept direction from Hanoi, it was also strongly anti-Sihanouk, and despite Hanoi's advice attempted to provoke a rural uprising against the Prince's rule.[45] Sihanouk struck back vigorously, however, and by the spring of 1970 the Party's armed forces had been reduced to a few hundred Cambodian guerrillas in the Northwest and in the Eastern provinces adjacent to South Vietnam, where Viet Cong units were operating in force.

The overthrow of Sihanouk and the invasion of Eastern Cambodia by South Vietnamese and American armed forces in April 1970 changed the situation drastically. At first the local Viet Cong leadership attempted to negotiate with the new government of General Lon Nol in an effort to maintain its supply route from the Cambodian seaport of Sihanoukville (soon to be renamed Kompong Som). Lon Nol refused, however, and gave the Vietnamese an ultimatum to remove their armed forces from Cambodian soil. At that point Hanoi decided to abandon its policy of maintaining a neutral Cambodia and build up the KCP for a full-scale military confrontation with the new government in Phnom Penh. Members of the KCP who had been living in the DRV were returned to Cambodia in an effort to give the movement experienced leadership and a pro-Hanoi point of view. To provide international respectability, Hanoi persuaded the KCP to accept Sihanouk, now living in Peking, as titular leader of a new National United Front for Kampuchea (FUNK), despite Pol Pot's deep dislike for the Prince. In April, a conference attended by representatives of the Communist Parties of Vietnam, Cambodia, and Laos was held in South China and agreed on the formation of a mutual alliance to drive imperialism out of Indochina.[46]

After 1970, communist operations in Cambodia gradually expanded from the border provinces westward toward the capital. While some of this success could be attributed to the growing strength of the Cambodian liberation armed forces (often called the Khmer Rouge), behind that success lay Vietnamese organizational methods. Viet Cong units in the area provided the relatively inexperienced Cambodians with military training and assistance in setting up a revolutionary apparatus at the village and hamlet level. From the outset, however, relations between the Vietnamese and the KCP leadeship were characterized by tension and distrust. The Pol Pot faction was suspicious of those members of the Party who had been trained in Hanoi, apparently convinced that they were part of a shadow organization set up in the DRV to replace the Pol Pot leadership and reestablish Vietnamese domination over the Cambodian revolutionary movement. As tensions rose, pro-Hanoi elements began to be purged from the Party. In the meantime, relations between the local Cambodian population and the Viet Cong units operating in the area began to deteriorate as increasing mutual contact seemed to feed suspicion and dislike which had historically marked the relations between the two peoples.[47]

Until the end of the war, open conflict between the two parties was avoided. Immediately following the return of peace, however, the tension broke out into the open. A few days after the fall of Saigon and Phnom Penh to communist forces, Khmer Rouge military units attacked Vietnamese border towns from the province of Tay Ninh, north of the Parrot's Beak, to Ha Tien on the Gulf of Thailand. Other forces from the mainland and the island of Poulo Wai in the Gulf launched assaults on the Vietnamese-held islands of Tho Chu (Poulo Panjang) and Phu Quoc, a larger island a few miles off the coast of Cambodia. The Vietnamese counterattacked and drove the invaders back to Poulu Wai, which they occupied briefly, only to withdraw a few weeks later.

At that time, the two sides were able to contain their animosity, and peace talks were convened to seek a negotiated settlement. But it soon became evident that the boundary dispute would not be easy to resolve. Discussions on the territorial issue had been held between the Sihanouk government and the National Liberation Front in 1964. At that time Phnom Penh had allegedly offered to abandon its territorial claims in South Vietnam (the lower provinces of the Mekong River, which had been seized and occupied by Vietnam two centuries earlier) in return for an unambiguous recognition by the NLF of the existing land border and acceptance of Cambodian claims over several offshore islands in the Gulf of Thailand.

In actuality, the differences over the land border, drawn up during French rule, were relatively minor. More important was the question of jurisdiction over the numerous small islands in the Gulf of Thailand, since Phnom Penh claimed ownership over several which were currently occupied and claimed by the South Vietnamese, including Tho Chu and others nearer the coast.

The dispute stemmed partly from the fact that ownership over the offshore islands had not been definitely settled under French rule. In 1939, French Governor-General Brevie had directed the drawing of a boundary line (from that time described as the Brevie Line) in the Gulf of Thailand south of the Protectorate of Cambodia and the Colony of Cochin-China. According to Brevie's instructions, the line was to be drawn "at right angles to the coast, at the frontier between Cambodia and Cochin-China, and making an angle of 140 (degrees) with the meridian north. . . ." This line, however, was not intended by the French to serve as a formal demarcation of the sea border. That remained uncertain:

> The administration and police powers with regard to these
> islands will therefore by clearly distributed to Cochinchina
> and Cambodia in order to avoid any dispute in the future.
> Of course, only the matters of administration and the police
> are considered here, the question of those [sic] territory
> these islands are remains outstanding.[48]

During the 1964 negotiations, the Sihanouk government had rejected the Brevie Line as a basis for a settlement of the sea border, claiming that acceptance of the Line would deprive Cambodia of ownership of several islands in the Gulf. According to a recent claim by Hanoi, the talks deadlocked on this issue. The two sides did agree, however, to accept the existing land border. When talks resumed in April 1976, the situation had changed, not only because of the new government in Phnom Penh but also because of the rising importance of the concept of the territorial sea as a source for national economic wealth. Hanoi, understandably concerned about the natural resources available in the Gulf, refused to accept the Brevie Line as the basis for a determination of the sea border between the two countries, but only with regard to sovereignty over the offshore islands. At the same time, the tentative agreement over the land border reached in 1965 now broke down under the extensive (Hanoi would say extravagant) claims made by the Pol Pot regime for the return of the lost territories in the lower Mekong. The extent of these claims, and the degree of emotional fervor underlying them, was graphically displayed in the so-called "Black Paper" issued by the Cambodian Ministry of Foreign Affairs in September 1978.[49] Once again, the talks were unable to resolve the territorial issue, and adjourned. Shortly afterward, the border conflict resumed. Available evidence suggests that the Pol Pot regime played the aggressive role, harassing Vietnamese settlements along the border, destroying combat villages and NEAs, and kidnapping or massacring the local inhabitants. In response, the Vietnamese began to strengthen their own military forces in the area, and occasionally launched counter-attacks of their own into Cambodia. In the meantime, the verbal war over the sea border continued. Hanoi tried to outflank Phnom Penh in May of 1977 by issuing a joint communique with Thailand on mutual claims over the territorial sea, and agreeing to settle any disagreements by peaceful means. A few days later Phnom Penh issued a claim of its own to a 200-mile economic zone which clashed in several respects with the claims made by Hanoi.

Behind the immediate issue of conflicting territorial claims lay Phnom Penh's persistent fear of Vietnamese domination. According to the Pol Pot regime, Hanoi was determined to dominate its neighbors through the formation of an Indochinese Federation. The Black Paper of 1978, subtitled "Facts and Evidences of the Acts of Aggression and Annexation of Vietnam Against Kampuchea," displays a shrill hatred of the Vietnamese and an almost hysterical fear of Hanoi's designs on Cambodian territory. Hanoi has categorically denied its intention to seek such a Federation, and remarks only that the shared fate of the three countries under imperialist rule shows the need for an "intimate relationship" in the future. As one high Vietnamese official remarked to a French journalist recently: "Naturally, we insist on special relations because we shared everything during the war."[50]

Vietnam's postwar relations with Laos stood in striking contrast to those with Democratic Kampuchea. Lacking a historical traditional of mutual animosity, the VWP and the Laotian People's Revolutionary Party had cooperated with relative cordiality during the war when thousands of Vietnamese troops had been stationed in Laos, most of them working on the Ho Chi Minh Trail. Soon after the end of the war in Vietnam and Cambodia in 1975, Laos made a peaceful transition to communist rule. In the postwar period Hanoi continued to maintain several thousand troops and advisers in the country, and in 1977 a Treaty of Friendship and Cooperation was signed between Hanoi and Vientiane. The maintenance of an "intimate relationship" with Vietnam was presumably

advantageous to the Laotians, at least in a material sense. It provided for
Vietnamese and Soviet economic and technical assistance and the presence of
over a thousand Soviet advisers. The relationship drew Laos more firmly
into the Soviet orbit, however, and thus brought into question its relations
with Peking. During the immediate postwar years the PRC maintained several
projects in Laos, notably a road system in the North near the Chinese border.
But China was undoubtedly concerned about the general trend in Laotian foreign
policy. There have been reports that several thousand pro-Chinese members of
the LPRP were purged in late 1975, presumably because they opposed the leadership's policy of close ties with Hanoi and Moscow. In 1978 Vientiane complained
that Peking was training mountain tribesmen in Northern Laos and instigating
them to revolt against the central government.[51]

Relations with ASEAN

One of the major effects of the border dispute with Cambodia was to com-
plicate Vietnam's relations with other states in the region. In the last
years of the war, these relations had been mixed. Five of the nations in
the area - Indonesia, Malaysia, Singapore, Thailand, and the Philippines -
had become associated in the Association for the Southeast Asian Nations
(ASEAN). The ASEAN alliance had tended to concentrate on issues of economic
and cultural cooperation because of the difficulty of coordinating attitudes
and policies in the area of regional and international politics. The war in
Vietnam had been a case in point. Some of the ASEAN states had adopted a
policy of strict neutrality in the conflict while others had provided verbal
or material support to the Saigon regime. Hanoi had retaliated by publicly
scorning ASEAN as a tool of American imperialist designs in Southeast Asia.

The fall of Indochina to the communists frightened the ASEAN nations
and suggestions were soon raised that the new states be invited to join the
alliance. At first, Vietnam appeared to express little interest in improving
relations with its neighbors and throughout much of the year repeated its
charge that ASEAN was a puppet of the American neo-colonialists. Hanoi's
main targets of criticism were Thailand and the Philippines, who were singled
out for permitting American bases on their soil.

In the early postwar period, then, there appeared no likelihood of an
immediate improvement in relations between Vietnam and the ASEAN states. For
the moment, the discord tended to center more on symbolic than on concrete
issues, on mutual distrust and a perceived inability to agree on acceptable
principles for the establishment of an amicable relationship. For several
years the ASEAN states had sponsored a concept calling for international recognition of Southeast Asia as a zone of peace, freedom and neutrality. After
the end of the Vietnam War the alliance proposed the zone in the United Nations,
and again at the 1976 summit meeting of the nonaligned nations held in Colombo.
At that time Vietnam was invited to add its support to the proposal. Hanoi,
however, was concerned that the term "freedom" could provide a basis for criticism of its policies in the area of human rights, and rejected the ASEAN formu-
lation, countering with a proposal of its own calling for a Southeast Asia
based on peace, neutrality, and independence. The concept of independence
was interpreted in terms of three principles: 1) opposition to all foreign
military bases in Southeast Asia, 2) independence and freedom of all countries

in Southeast Asia, and 3) peaceful and friendly relations between all countries in the region. Clearly, the Vietnamese proposal could not be acceptable to several of the ASEAN nations, and indicated that for the moment, Hanoi was not interested in a serious examination of mutual interests with its non-communist neighbors in the region.

The ASEAN states, however, continued their efforts to assure Hanoi that the alliance was not a military association directed against Vietnam or the other new communist governments in Indochina. Finally, in the summer of 1976, Hanoi made its first public conciliatory gesture when Foreign Minister Nguyen Duy Trinh added a fourth principle to the three included in the original Vietnamese proposal. The new point called for mutual cooperation in promoting prosperity in keeping with each country's specific conditions.[52] Shortly after, Trinh's deputy Phan Hien made an extensive tour of Southeast Asia, including most of the ASEAN capitals. Hien's attitude was conciliatory, but he made it clear that Vietnam continued to oppose the ASEAN proposal for a zone of peace and indicated that the presence of American military bases was the major obstacle to better relations with the alliance. For its part, ASEAN continued its own efforts and in August 1977 issued a joint communique stressing its desire for "peaceful and mutual beneficial relations with all countries in the region."

Relations with Thailand

Among the individual ASEAN states, the one most directly concerned with the implications of the communist victory in Vietnam was Thailand. Bangkok's historic suspicion of Hanoi's long-term objectives in Southeast Asia and its fear of possible Vietnamese support for the insurgency movement within its own borders had been contributing factors leading the Thai government to support American policy in South Vietnam during the war. In turn, such support had hardened Vietnamese antagonism towards Thailand, which was viewed in Hanoi as the chief puppet of American imperialism in Southeast Asia. The end of the war, coupled with the rise of a new civilian government in Thailand after the 1973 revolution, offered an opportunity for reconciliation. The new government in Bangkok had expressed its determination to remove the American military presence in Thailand and adopt a more neutralist stance in regional affairs. This in turn appeared to open the door for a rapprochement between the two long-time rivals, and a Vietnamese delegation went to Bangkok to discuss the restoration of normal relations. The Thai were receptive to a Vietnamese proposal for a set of principles to govern their mutual relations, calling for: 1) mutual respect for the independence, sovereignty, and territorial integrity of each party, 2) agreement by both parties not to allow any foreign country to use their territory as a base for direct or indirect aggression against the other states in the area, and 3) the establishment of friendly and neighborly relations, including agreements for economic and cultural exchange. The agreement broke down, however, on another issue, as Thailand refused to agree to Hanoi's demand to return aircraft flown to Thailand by South Vietnamese pilots seeking exile, and the talks were adjourned without a final agreement.[53]

The negotiations had shown that there was some desire for an improvement in relations on both sides but real issues, exacerbated by a continued high degree of mutual suspicion, continued to intervene. Bangkok complained that Vietnam was training Thai guerrillas in Laos and infiltrating them across the Mekong for operations in Thailand, and pointed to the Vietnam-Lao joint communique of February 11, 1976, which had noted that the two signatories "totally support the struggle of the Thai people for a truly independent democratic Thailand without U.S. military bases," as evidence that Hanoi was not sincere in its protestations that it had no intention of supporting the subversive movement in Thailand. For its part, Hanoi denied the accusation and noted the glacial pace of the withdrawal of American forces from Thailand. It also complained that Vietnamese residents in Thailand were being singled out for persecution.

In August of 1976 talks resumed and resulted in a joint communique calling for an exchange of ambassadors and the opening of negotiations on trade and economic cooperation. In a gesture designed to defuse one of the main sources of tension, the SRV agreed to establish a joint committee for the repatriation of Vietnamese refugees in Thailand. It also dropped its demand for the return of South Vietnamese aircraft flown to Bangkok. In October, however, a military coup overthrew the civilian government of Kukrit Pramoj and brought to power a new military government less sympathetic to the communist experiment in Vietnam. At first Hanoi reacted harshly, claiming that the "reactionary" coup had been staged by the United States. Vietnam was particularly critical of indications that the new Thai government might be more receptive to a continued American military presence than its predecessor, and at one point even issued an ominous warning that Washington's policies in Thailand were following the same path that they had followed in Vietnam, leading inexorably to the same disastrous results. When it became clear that the new Thai government, though more friendly to the United States, wished to pursue talks designed to improve relations with Vietnam, contacts resumed. In May 1977 a conference was held between Vietnam, Thailand and Laos to consider the resurrection of the Makong Development Project, which had been killed by the Vietnam War. While little of substance came from the talks, there was agreement to reconvene at a later date, and Hanoi gave private assurances of its sincere interest in the project.

The Nationalization of Industry in the South

Throughout 1976 and 1977 Vietnamese economic planners made a major effort to restore the national economy to a peacetime footing and permit the fulfillment of the ambitious goals of the Five-Year Plan. But the Party leadership was now discovering that the problems of peace could be as intractable as those of war. Much of the problem was structural. The economy was still based primarily on small-scale production. The infrastructure was still primitive and the technological level of the population was low. Most government and party cadres lacked managerial experience and many were proving susceptible to corruption and the temptations of bourgeois society in the South. Even in the North there were distressing signs of slackness, sluggishness, and inefficiency.

It was, of course, one of the objectives of the Five-Year Plan to overcome such problems. In fact, however, the Plan soon began to run into serious difficulties. Part of the problem arose from the fact that the country was forced to rely on foreign assistance for a large proportion of its basic needs. Yet even here the regime ran into difficulties, for although the level of aid from abroad was substantial, the country had trouble in absorbing it. Bureaucratic red tape and a lack of equipment and stevedores hindered the unloading of goods at seaports and created bottlenecks in Haiphong, Saigon and Da Nang. An inadequate rail network and a lack of trucks (according to one 1977 report, nearly one-third of all trucks in Vietnam were out of operation because of a lack of spare parts) hampered the movement of goods from dockside to their point of destination. Within the industrial sector, poor managerial techniques and a lack of qualified technicians reduced production and caused a number of major projects, including a major steel mill supported by Swedish assistance at Thai Nguyen, to be cut back, postponed, or even abandoned.

In South Vietnam the economic infrastructure was somewhat more advanced than in the North, and there was an adequate pool of trained technological experts. Here, however, the regime was hampered by its lack of control over the urban economy. For the moment, it had decided to move cautiously in order to encourage private business to invest its capital, equipment, and expertise in the task of nation building. In some instances, however, the government moved directly to take control over an entire sector of the economy. During the campaign against the comprador bourgeoisie in 1975 and 1976, the stranglehold of private capital over the distribution of rice, wholesale meat, fish and vegetables, and gasoline had been broken. A number of other major areas such as communications and transport, printing, hotels and landlord housing, fertilizers and insecticides, pharmaceuticals, textiles and chemical products were fully nationalized.[54] In other cases, the Party had turned to the standard transitional organization, the joint state-private enterprise. As described in a <u>Nhan Dan</u> editorial, these enterprises were

> originally private enterprises which have been placed under
> the joint management of the state and their original owners
> or representatives, and which receive additional capital
> invested by the state. The state will play a leading role
> in these enterprises while the legal interests of private
> shareholders will be protected and the basic interests of the
> workers and personnel guaranteed.[55]

In general, small trade and manufacturing in the South remained in private hands. According to one government report there were still about 400 private factories and nearly 15,000 small businesses and handicraft shops under private ownership, accounting for about 65% of total industrial porduction. As might be expected, the juxtaposition of private enterprise and Marxist bureaucracy was not always felicitous. The natural distrust of technicians and officials of the old regime by Party Cadres hindered cooperative efforts, despite the blandishments of the government, and prompted one official publication to warn cadres against an overly restrictive view.

Cadres were admonished not to judge an individual solely on the basis of his past activities and class background, but also to take into account his recent struggles and personal commitments.[56]

In some respects, the price for gradualism was severe. Hoarding and price speculation caused shortages of consumer goods and rising prices for most commodities, although foreign observers reported that shops were better stocked in South Vietnam than in the North. Unemployment, too, remained a serious problem. Despite the considerable efforts of the government which had created nearly half a million new jobs, the rate of unemployment in Ho Chi Minh City remained at nearly two million. Some of the excess had been absorbed by resettlement on the new NEAs (according to one government estimate, there were over 750,000 residents in the settlements by the end of 1977), but problems were still being encountered in transforming the settlements into attractive alternatives to urban life, and many residents were reportedly streaming back into the cities.[57]

Similar problems were being encountered in the agricultural sector. For the time being, the regime had decided to resist the temptation to collectivize the countryside in order to encourage farmers in the South to increase food production and end the chronic food shortage which had plagued the DRV throughout its brief history. Programs were set up to encourage double-cropping and the development of subsidiary crops. Units of the PAVN were assigned to help villagers in water conservancy projects and the clearing of virgin lands. A major program was launched to construct a green belt around Ho Chi Minh City which could relieve the city's traditional dependency on Dalat for its vegetable needs.

Through such efforts the regime had hoped to achieve substantial increases in agricultural production during the period of the Five-Year Plan. From the beginning, however, such expectations were disappointed. As is so often the case, part of the problem was the consequence of unpredictable weather. In 1976 and 1977 the familiar demons of flood and drought caused severe crop damage. Grain losses in 1976 allegedly reached over two million metric tons. The following year typhoons in Central Vietnam and unusually cold weather in the North kept the grain harvest even smaller.

The problem was compounded by the unwillingness of farmers in the South to sell their grain to state purchasing organizations at the artificially low official price. According to one estimate, 600,000 tons of padi were kept off the market, forcing the government to use its scarce foreign currency reserves to import heavily from abroad, chiefly from the Soviet Union. Even so, the food supply was well short of needs and grain rationing had to be introduced. According to reports, rice consumption in the North fell as low as 15 kilograms per adult per month, barely adequate for subsistence.[58]

Under the circumstances, it is hardly surprising that the perceptible sense of malaise which had afflicted Vietnamese society since the end of the war continued to cause serious concern to the communist regime. Cadres and ordinary citizens alike appeared increasingly immune to the familiar appeals to patriotism, hard work and personal sacrifice which had served the Party

over three decades of struggle against enemies at home and abroad. In early
1978, the Party revived Resolution 228, originally issued by the Politburo in
1974 against "negative aspects in socio-economic life" in an effort to raise
the quality of cadres. People's inspection committees were set up at the
grassroots level and the masses were called upon to register complaints against
official abuses. Although a number of officials were arrested and prosecuted
as a result of such procedures, in general the results were meager, since the
population, fearing reprisals, was often afraid to complain.

Whether such difficulties compelled the regime to revise its schedule
for transforming the Southern economy is a matter of dispute. Some Western
observers have speculated that the decision to nationalize trade and collectivize the rural areas beginning in 1978 reflected an acceleration of the
original plan. Communist observers deny this and point to the original goals
of the Plan as announced at the Fourth Party Congress in December 1976 (which
had directed that the transformation should be completed "in the main" by
1980) as evidence that the transformation of the South took place basically
on schedule. The truth of the matter cannot be determined here. What is
certain is that to Party planners, a major part of their problem lay in the
absence of sufficient government control over the economy in the South, a
condition that led to hoarding of goods, price gouging, and a flourishing
black market in the cities, and a shortage of grain in rural areas.

In any event, the decision to launch the first major step in the process
of transformation to socialist ownership in the South was apparently taken
at the Second Plenum of the Central Committee in June of 1977. An early
indication of the Party's intentions came in July when Le Duan announced
that the government would soon seize control over industry and commerce in
South Vietnam, and that collectives in rural areas would soon follow, first
in the suburban districts around Ho Chi Minh City and then, by the beginning
of 1979, on a larger scale throughout the region as a whole. To facilitate
the process the Central Committee established a Committee for the Transformation of Industry and Trade in South Vietnam under the chairmanship of Politburo member Nguyen Van Linh. In early August, the committee held a public
conference in Ho Chi Minh City to acquaint local cadres with the objectives
of the program. An August 4 editorial in Nhan Dan noted that the major
goals would be 1) to abolish capitalist production and the private control of
production and distribution, 2) to nationalize the means of production in its
various forms, and 3) to thereby create conditions for rural collectivization
and the socialist transformation of petty bourgeois commerce and handicrafts.
There was a note of caution: the editorial promised that the Party would
not "hastily effect the transformation of a large area without thorough
preparations."[59]

The first stage of the program, launched in the fall of 1977, was designed to effect the transformation by gradual means, but apparently had only
limited results. An editorial published in Nhan Dan the following March
complained that the transformation of private trade in the South had fallen
behind requirements and plans, and noted that the commercial bourgeoisie
(most of whom, according to the article, still showed "negative effects" and
cling to their "selfish interests") was still competing with the state trade

sector in the purchase of commodities, especially in agricultural products,
thus driving up prices and disrupting the market. In February, 1978,
Nguyen Van Linh was replaced as chairman of the Committee by his deputy and
alternative Politburo member Do Muoi.[60]

On March 23, 1978, the government acted, with a surprise announcement by
the chairman of the Ho Chi Minh City People's Committee that from that time
on all bourgeois elements were prohibited from carrying out commercial activities and were encouraged to join in socialist enterprises, to form joint
private-state organizations or to shift to productive activities. Only small
private traders who "live by their labor and play a role in goods distribution" were allowed to continue private operations. As an added incentive
to businessmen, the government promised to provide assistance in providing
training for new employment.

The previous effort to seize control of the property of the comprador
bourgeoisie soon after the communist seizure of power had been thwarted when
businessmen in Cholon (where, regime sources conceded, the control system did
not operate effectively), were able to manage a last-minute dispersal of
goods among friends and relatives. To avoid a repetition, the authorities
now mobilized thousands of youth assault squads (supplemented in some instances by
units of the PAVN) the night before the announcement to raid private shops and
undertake an inventory of stocks. The announcement made the following day
declared that all requisitioned goods would be purchased (at cost, plus 10%
profit) by the state if the owner could provide a bill of sale. Since the
official price was usually well below the actual market price, and so many
goods had been obtained through black market channels, many businessmen were
ruined.[61]

The confiscation of private stocks was accompanied by new currency measures limiting the amount of money which citizens could retain for their own
use. Amounts above the legal limit had to be placed in savings accounts
and could only be used after application to the government authorities. In
May a new unified currency was issued for all of Vietnam. New banknotes
appeared and the old ones (the Southern dong) were withdrawn. South Vietnamese
citizens were permitted to exchange old notes for the new currency but, unlike
1975, a limit was imposed on withdrawals. In early April, additional moves
were taken against remaining private firms, not only in the South but also in
the North, where it had been permitted to exist under the pressure of wartime
conditions. There was a crackdown on open-air markets selling stolen goods,
while individuals involved in private commerce were required to conform to
rigid state regulations and production guidelines and agree to sign contracts
to sell their products to the state.[62]

Technically speaking, the program appeared to be a success. Within a few
days, nearly all major merchants in South Vietnam had completed the necessary
procedures and by summer, according to government reports, some 30,000 private
businesses had closed their doors, leading Do Muoi, chairman of the Committee
on the Transformation of Private Industry and Trade, to declare that private
commerce in the South had been "basically destroyed." Of those who abandoned
their private operations, some shifted to productive activities or joined

private-state or collective enterprises. Those who did not reinvest their capital were apparently pressed to settle on NEAs. The remaining private entrepreneurs in Vietnam, observed chairman Do Muoi, were largely "medium and small types," who would be persuaded to abandon their activities by "voluntary means."[63]

The decision to launch the transition to socialism in South Vietnam less than three years after the fall of the GVN represented a major gamble by the regime and it is not surprising that there were hints in the official press of dissent within the high councils of the Party. An April 1st editorial in Nhan Dan commented that

> some people contend that integrated revolution, socialism and the abolition of the capitalist economy are not neces-sary, that socialism can set good examples while overcoming its own shortcomings and that the good points of capitalism and private economic systems can be of use. Realities in the past three years have adequately exposed the vegative [sic] aspects of these two economic systems. Although being gradually limited and restricted to a very small area, the capitalist economy has continued to "rule the roost." So long as it exists, the reorganization of agriculture and handicrafts along socialist lines will be very difficult. Similarly, as long as capitalist trade survives, it will be impossible to build a strong socialist trade.[64]

The Collectivization of Agriculture

Statements in the Party press had made it clear that the transformation of industry and commerce in the South was viewed as a preparatory step toward the collectivization of the countryside. The abolition of private commerce would provide the state with control over the distribution of food and consumer goods. With more of the latter available, and at a lower price, the regime could then hope to entice farmers to sell their rice to state purchasing agencies, and give serious consideration to the benefits of socialism.

Until 1978 there had been few efforts to establish socialist relations in the Southern countryside. There were occasional references in the media to the formation of experimental collectives and state farms, but it was evident that such developments represented the exception rather than the rule. As for official statements, little had been said beyond the declaration at the Fourth Party Congress that collectivization in the South should be "basically completed" by the end of the 1976-1980 Five-Year Plan.

There were signs, however, that changes were on the horizon. Not long after the fall of Saigon, a major campaign was launched to promote the forma-tion of limited cooperative ventures for peasants in the area of planting and harvesting. Traditionally such organizations have been considered as the first step in the socialization process in the countryside (one source described them as "a short and preparatory stage which is, however, very necessary"). In Vietnam, they took a variety of forms depending on the

particular local circumstances. According to official sources, there were
basically two types: 1) work exchange teams and production solidarity teams
and 2) production collectives and cooperative labor teams. Work exchange
and production solidarity teams were described in the press as cooperative
labor teams at the hamlet level which establish contractual relations with
the authorities for production goals, but do not collectivize the means of
production such as farm land, machinery, and draft animals. Some of these
teams were established on a permanent basis, while others were irregular in
operation, taking form usually at peak working periods in the harvest cycle.

The production collectives (or, alternatively, the cooperative labor
teams) were actually small cooperatives. The basic means of production within
the organization would be socialized, and the teams would produce according to
established plans. They were smaller in size than the usual collective, however, normally consisting of 60 to 70 farm families working on a cultivated
area of 30 to 35 hectares. One source described the production collectives
as "small cooperatives whose scope it is to collectivize production materials
as a development step toward cooperatives."[65]

It is clear from official press reports that the production collectives
were considered to be the higher form, and were to be established in preference to the work exchange teams and production solidarity teams, wherever
that was appropriate. In general production collectives were formed in areas
where political awareness was high (much of the coastal region of Central
Vietnam, for example), or where there was much public land, wasteland, or
reclaimed land (as in the Central Highlands and on NEAs). The lower forms,
considered easier for peasants to accept, were constructed primarily in those
areas where there was a high proportion of private land-holding peasants and
little sympathy for the revolution, as in the lower provinces of the Mekong
Dalta. In these areas, only a few production collectives were initially
established, and most were on public land.

The decision to move towards the second stage of the socialization process
in rural areas - the construction of collective farms - was made at the Second
Plenum held in the summer of 1977. In September a Committee for the Transformation of Southern Agriculture was set up under the chairmanship of veteran
Party leader Vo Chi Cong. Lower-level committees soon began to appear at
province and district levels. Each province was instructed to establish
pilot cooperatives in selected districts by the winter of 1977-1978. To provide experienced leadership, teams composed of cadres from North Vietnam were
designated to establish schools in each province for training Southern cadres
in the collectivization process. All in all, the timing of the process
appeared to reflect the guidelines earlier established by the Fourth Party
Congress: "basically achieve the establishment of socialist production relations in the Southern countryside by the first years of the 1980s."

At the end of November, the Committee held its first conference in Ho
Chi Minh City to consider measures to accelerate the process of forming
work   exchange teams, production solidarity teams, and production collectives, and to create an administrative mechanism at the district level to
begin the formation of collectives in the South. At that moment, approximately one million peasants were enrolled in the various types of work-sharing

teams, and a few pilot collectives had been established in selected districts.
As emphasized in a speech by Chairman Vo Chi Cong, the goal was to complete the
process of building full-scale collectives throughout Central Vietnam by the
end of the Five-Year Plan in 1980. By the beginning of that year, peasants
in the Mekong Delta should be fully enrolled in production collectives, and
begin the transition to full collectivization.[66]

As in the case of the earlier stage of work-sharing organizations, the
pace of collectivization varied with the circumstances in the particular area.
In provinces or districts where conditions were favorable, the process was
fairly rapid. In the Mekong Delta, where resistance to collectivization by
well-to-do peasants was expected to be strong, it was considerably slower. The
statistics reflect the story. By mid-August of 1978 there were 132 agricultural collectives in South Vietnam. Of the total, 108 were located along the
Central coast, nineteen were in the Central Highlands, two were in the provinces northeast of Ho Chi Minh City, two were in the Mekong Delta, and one was
in Ho Chi Minh City suburbs. Nearly 80 of the collectives had been built from
production collectives, while 54 had emerged from work exchange teams or production solidarity teams.[67] In general, the regime hoped to rely on persuasion
rather than on force, in the hope of reducing resistance and increasing
production. According to Hoang Tung, editor of Nhan Dan:

> One of the chief principles of our Party holds that the
> peasantry must be reorganized in a rational fashion, then
> production will not decrease but rather will increase.
> When carrying out collectivization we take great care not
> to turn the middle peasant against us. In the course of
> collectivization we rely exclusively on persuasion . . .
> We are trying to get at least 90 percent of the peasantry
> to join the cooperative movement. If we tried for less,
> then the middle and rich peasants would not join the move-
> ment and in this case competition would develop between the
> producer cooperatives and the private farmers. We want to
> avoid this at all costs. It is also our goal to make
> available to the peasants suitable tools for cultivating
> the land. We are buying or renting the animals (primarily
> buffaloes) and tractors which are privately owned as well
> as pumps and other tools. We would not like to repeat
> cases such as happened in some provinces. Some overzealous
> leaders organized five producer cooperatives [production
> collectives: author] in a single province instead of the
> recommended one or two and the result was that the peasants
> slaughtered their draft animals en masse. The party ordered
> that producer cooperatives created against the wishes of the
> peasants should be disbanded. We must carry out the econ-
> omic policy such that the great majority of the peasantry
> will join the cooperatives movement voluntarily.[68]

The various forms of the collectives appeared to be as diverse as had
been the case with the work-sharing teams. According to government reports,
the majority were full collectives which have "thoroughly collectivized the

means of production," including rice fields, buffalo and cattle, and machinery. And, according to a speech by Vo Chi Cong at a conference held in August of 1978, there were a variety of arrangements and facilities within the new organizations. Some have set up medical and sanitation facilities, kindergartens and day care centers. Some have achieved collectivization in conjunction with land reform (based on regulations confiscating all land in excess of family requirements and distributing it to the poor) while in other cases, reform was accomplished previously or was not necessary. Finally, some combined the process with the formation of agro-industrial centers at the district level.

The new organizations soon began to run into problems. One was structural. In his speech at the August conference, Vo Chi Cong remarked that many of the new collective organizations were too large, given the managerial weaknesses of most of the cadres. Noting that some of the collectives consisted of nearly 1,000 hectares of land, he suggested that for the time being, they should be limited to no more than 200 hectares. Later, when managerial deficiencies had been remedied, they could be increased to an optimum size of 300 to 400 hectares.

A second and potentially more dangerous problem concerned the techniques being used to persuade peasants to join the collectives. While statements in the official press remarked with satisfaction that over 90% of the villagers in many areas had volunteered to join the new organizations, other government sources noted with concern that cadres frequently used threats or administrative measures to compel reluctant peasants to join. One report noted that where less than 90 percent of the local inhabitants had failed to volunteer, cadres often "use harsh language in order to threaten the peasants" and obtain compliance.[69]

Unfortunately for the regime, the beginning of the program to transform production relations in the countryside coincided with another spell of bad weather. In the summer of 1978 the Central coast was hit with the biggest floods on record. Over three million tons of rice and half a million houses were destroyed. The total rice crop was only 10.5 million metric tons, well short of basic needs. To make things worse farmers, put off by low official prices, continued to hold back rice and use it to make liquor or to raise pigs and ducks. To provide incentives for farmers to increase production, the government issued new regulations allowing individuals to cultivate land unused by the collectives and enjoy the harvest in full. Virgin or reclaimed land could be cultivated for three to five years without payment of agricultural taxes.

Like the decision to nationalize industry, the move to collectivize agriculture in the South created tensions within the Party leadership over the pace of change. An article by Hoang Tung in the February 1978 issue of Tap Chi Cong San noted that "some fear that we are going too fast to large-scale production" and confirmed that the pace of collectivization would be more rapid than in the North over two decades earlier. But there was no choice, added Tung, for in the absence of collectivization, rich and middle peasants would control the rural economy and set back the advance of the revolution.

Not all agreed. By mid-summer the struggle within the leadership had reached
near-crisis proportions. One editorial in the Party newspaper defended the
decision to collectivize and pointed out that "socialism is characterized by
principles and objective laws of which the vital one is the Dictatorship of
the Proletariat built on the system of public ownership of the means of production and unified and centralized management on the basis of democracy."
Nhan Dan criticized unnamed Party members who showed weakness in the face of
difficulties, and implied that some "have succumbed midway and some bad elements have sold themselves to the aggressors." It hinted that others might
join the ranks of the enemy and noted defensively that "no Party has been able
to avoid losses and betrayal by some people."[70]

The Chinese Exodus

One of the most important consequences of the campaign to abolish private
trade was the weakening of the economic power and influence of the overseas
Chinese community in Vietnam. Out of a total of over one and a half million
ethnic Chinese residing in the country, all but about 200,000 lived in the
South, where for generations they had dominated the bulk of the wholesale
trade, banking and much of the retail trade of South Vietnam. Ethnic Chinese
in the North were involved in commerce, fishing, mining, factory work, and
even in farming. Throughout recent history, first under the native monarchy
and later under the French, the Chinese had retained their separate legal
and cultural status in Vietnam. After the Geneva Accords, however, efforts
were undertaken by the governments in both zones to resolve the problem.
The regime of Ngo Dinh Diem in Saigon attempted to compel ethnic Chinese
to assimilate by requiring all residents engaged in commercial activities
to take out Vietnamese citizenship. Although most elected to become Vietnamese
citizens, the Chinese community as a whole continued to maintain their own
separate schools and their distinctive way of life. In the North the communists moved with greater circumspection. In 1955 Hanoi reached an agreement
with Peking to encourage Chinese nationals to adopt Vietnamese citizenship on
a gradual and voluntary basis. Throughout the next two decades, despite some
evidence of official irritation at the lack of commitment by ethnic Chinese
to the war effort (and some suspicion of their underlying loyalty to Peking),
the regime held to its conciliatory policy. It permitted the continued
existence of Chinese schools and a limited degree of cultural autonomy. It
allowed many Chinese nationals to maintain their Chinese citizenship and did
not compel them to register for military service. And it tolerated the
survival of a small private commercial sector, dominated by the Chinese
community in Hanoi and Haiphong.

The end of the war did not immediately bring substantive changes to the
situation. Chinese businessmen were permitted to remain in private operations
and Chinese schools in the South were permitted to remain open after the obli-
gatory period of faculty and staff reindoctrination. Under the surface, however, there were clear indications that the regime did not look favorably on
the ethnic Chinese in the South. By implication, the campaign against the
comprador bourgeoisie was directed against the Chinese community in Cholon.
Twelve of the fifteen entrepreneurs arrested for economic crimes against the
people in 1975 were of Chinese extraction. Reports in the press indicated

that a high proportion of those Southerners compelled to resettle in the NEAs were Chinese. Official sources conceded that the regime was experiencing some difficulty in dealing with the Chinese community, citing such problems as open air traders, the hoarding of raw materials, counter-revolutionary activities and "feudal attitudes."

Whether or not the move to nationalize commerce in South Vietnam was viewed by the regime as a means of getting rid of the ethnic Chinese is unclear. Many refugee sources claim that a decision to that effect was taken at a special conference called by Party leaders in the summer of 1977, and that public security officers were forewarned at that time to prepare for a campaign to persecute the local Chinese. Other observers are convinced that the Party leaders did not deliberately intend to antagonize the Hoa (as the Chinese are called in Vietnam), at least until 1978. At that time, most accounts agree that a special bureau within the public security apparatus was designated to facilitate departures.[71]

Whatever the truth of the matter, the Chinese community was clearly the victim of several forces beyond its control - the decision by the Hanoi regime to move toward socialism in the South, the worsening relations between China and Vietnam, compounded by the age-old hostility between the two people that had never quite subsided during a generation of wartime alliance. The exodus appears to have begun sometime in 1977 in the North. Chinese merchants noted an increase in visits by tax officials and security agents. Rumors began to circulate that the government was preparing to take measures against the local Chinese community and compel them all to join in the new agricultural settlements. According to reports, some were indeed forced to settle in NEAs and a few who had refused to take out Vietnamese citizenship were allegedly encouraged unofficially to leave. With food short, low pay, and rising conscription rates, many were attracted by reports that life was better in China, and increasing numbers began to sell their property and flee across the land border into the PRC. Available evidence suggests that at first, the exodus was apparently not tolerated or encouraged by the government. Hanoi radio reported that youth squads along the border had been instructed to apprehend potential refugees and confiscate their goods and money. In the wake of the nationalization of commerce in the spring of 1978, however, the flood of refugees into China reached sizeable proportions. In late May alone, over 17,000 left, bring the total for the year to nearly 100,000.[72] Many of those fleeing were dockworkers, fishermen and merchants. According to one report, nearly two-thirds of the entire Chinese population of the port city of Haiphong had left for China.

Criticism of Hanoi's responsibility for the crisis was soon forthcoming. In April Liao Ch'eng-chih, chairman of the Overseas Chinese Affairs Commission in Peking, complained of the maltreatment of the Hoa population in Vietnam. In May, the Chinese Foreign Ministry registered an official complaint, contending that Hanoi was deliberately mistreating Chinese citizens and had reneged on the 1955 agreement which had called for gradual and voluntary integration of ethnic Chinese into Vietnamese society.[73]

The Vietnamese countercharged that the flight of the Chinese had been incited by rumors deliberately provoked by Chinese Embassy officials in Vietnam. According to Hanoi, the Chinese government had all along viewed the _Hoa_ residing in Vietnam as Chinese nationals and had attempted to organize them in the interests of Chinese foreign policy. During the Cultural Revolution, Hanoi charged, China organized "core forces" among the ethnic Chinese "to stage a rebellion in this country" and incited youths of Chinese extraction to study Maotsetung Thought and organize a Red Guard Army. Now it was attempting to organize scout units, reconnaissance groups and a so-called "mountaineer division" among the upland minorities on the Vietnamese side of the border for use in a possible future conflict with Vietnam. As far as Chinese criticism of the confiscation of the property of ethnic Chinese in the South was concerned, Hanoi retorted that it was only doing what all communist governments, including the PRC itself, must do during the process of transition to socialism. Why, asked Hanoi, does Peking not inquire into the fate of the several hundred thousand Chinese merchants in Cambodia many of whom had not only been deprived of their livelihood, but their lives, by the vicious Pol Pot regime?[74]

In May the crisis deepened. There is some evidence from refugee sources that as tension between China and Vietnam increased, the authorities became increasingly suspicious of local Chinese, and many were dismissed from their jobs or ordered to resettle in NEAs. Some were arrested and charged with seditious acts and spreading rumors among the local population. Refugee accounts imply that there may have been some basis for official distrust of the underlying loyalties of ethnic Chinese in Vietnam. When war broke out many, even in the North, had a tendency to sympathize with China.[75] With the government now approving legal departures, long waiting lines appeared in front of the Chinese embassy as worried _Hoa_ attempted to obtain exit visas or proof of Chinese citizenship. Peking requested permission to open a consulate in Ho Chi Minh City to facilitate the process, but Hanoi refused. In retaliation, the PRC closed three Vietnamese consulates in South China. On May 27th, Peking announced that it intended to dispatch two ships to Vietnam to pick up those ethnic Chinese wishing to leave. Vietnam protested this as a "blatant act" and a violation of territorial sovereignty. When the ships arrived off the harbors of Haiphong and Vung Tau, negotiations commenced, but soon bogged down over procedures.

By late July, over 140,000 had fled to China. Most were settled on communes, either in the border provinces of Yunnan and Kwangsi or in Fukien, the province of origin of many of the refugees. Reports filtering back indicated that some found it difficult to adjust to conditions in China, and many urban residents were reluctant to engage in manual labor on farms. In exasperation, Peking closed the border and accused Vietnam of sending spies and other "bad elements" to cause trouble in China's southern provinces. It claimed that Hanoi had violated a joint "border control accord" calling for the passage only of individuals with official repatriation certificates at official check points.[76]

By late summer, the flow to China had temporarily been halted. Almost simultaneously, however, a massive exodus by sea began from the South. Thousands of refugees, mostly of Chinese origin, but including some native

Vietnamese unhappy with life under communism, departed by ship to seek refuge in neighboring countries. On arrival abroad, many indicated that their departure had been facilitated and in some cases even promoted by government officials. According to such reports, arrangements were often made with the formal approval of the local chief of police although actual procedures for the voyage were usually undertaken by middlemen. Travel would be either by junk or freighter (junks were cheaper, but did not depart on a regular schedule), and transportation could be arranged through official channels. The standard charge for the voyage (including permission to emigrate) was ten taels of gold (U.S. $2,000) for an adult, and half price for a child. Ethnic Vietnamese were expected to pay more, and a surcharge was often added on to cover transportation from the interior to the departure point, usually one of the smaller fishing ports in the Mekong Delta. Frequently it was necessary to provide additional kickbacks for the local officials. The Vietnamese government vehemently denied that it was officially charging refugees, but conceded that some corrupt officials were accepting bribes.[77]

Whatever the degree of Hanoi's complicity, the exodus of the "boat people" soon became a massive world problem and, for many, a human tragedy. The total number reaching foreign shores rapidly attained several hundred thousand, most of whom were destined to spend weeks or even months in crowded and unsanitary refugee camps on small islands off the coast of Malaysia or Indonesia. To make it worse, those who arrived were the lucky ones. Many others not so fortunate died at sea in storms or at the hands of pirates. In one reported case a boat seeking refuge in the Philippines ran aground on a reef in the Spratly Islands in the middle of the South China Sea. Vietnamese troops occupying one of the islands nearby spotted the refugees and shot at them. Only a handful managed to escape.

As the flood increased, several of the governments in the area, many of whom had severe political and social problems in assimilating their own Chinese nationals, became alarmed and refused to accept future arrivals. A few ships loaded with refugees were refused shelter and towed back out to sea. Under the pressure of circumstances, a conference attended by 30 nations was convened at Geneva in an effort to find a solution to a human problem of momentous proportions. At the conference there was open criticism of Vietnamese official complicity in the crisis, but Hanoi predictably refused to accept full responsibility. Claiming that the majority of those who wished to leave were middle class Chinese and Vietnamese used to the "high life" and unwilling to make personal sacrifices, it contended that some owed "blood debts" to the people and the regime had exercised "rare humanity" in permitting them to depart.[78]

The Break with China

In May, 1978, with relations between China and Vietnam continuing to deteriorate, Peking announced a cutback in its aid program to Vietnam, cancelling 21 aid projects currently underway. In July, it cancelled all 72 remaining projects and withdrew Chinese technicians from the country. The refugee issue was undoubtedly one factor in the souring of relations between Hanoi and Peking, and it may have been the _cause célèbre_ which provoked China into cutting

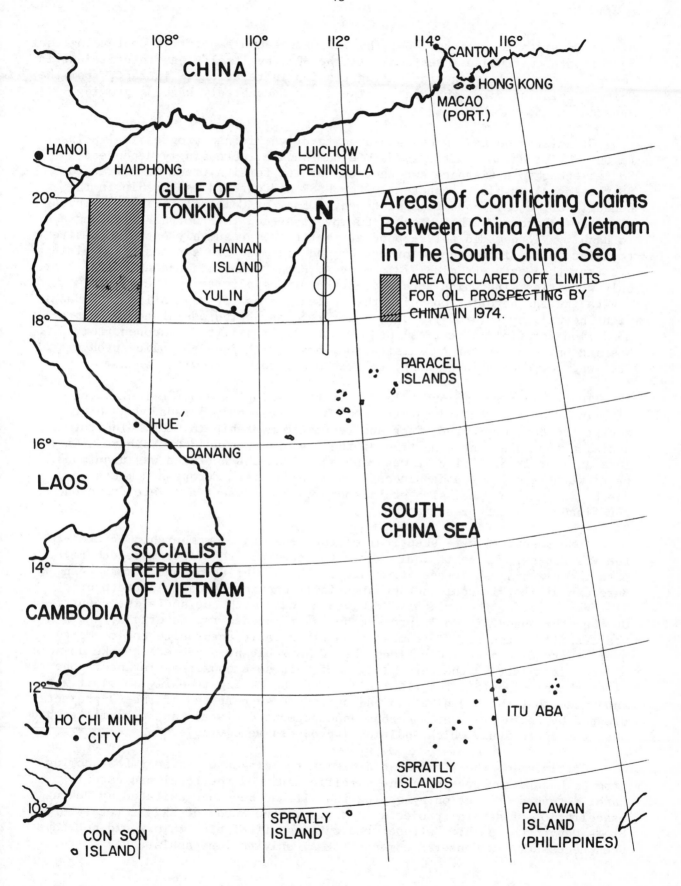

Areas Of Conflicting Claims Between China And Vietnam In The South China Sea

AREA DECLARED OFF LIMITS FOR OIL PROSPECTING BY CHINA IN 1974.

off its assistance program. But the Vietnamese had a point in contending that the dispute over Chinese residents in the SRV, by itself, was insufficient in importance to justify the increasing tension in relations. In fact, from the Chinese point of view, the central issue was undoubtedly Hanoi's growing dependence upon Moscow.

Circumstances had indeed appeared to drive Vietnam progressively closer to the Soviet Union. After 1975, Vietnam became increasingly dependent on Soviet economic assistance and the bulk of its foreign trade was directed to the socialist bloc. Apparently the USSR had offered membership in the Council for Mutual Economic Assistance, (CEMA, or Comecon) in 1976 during a visit by Politburo member Michael Suslov to attend the Fourth Party Congress in Hanoi. Vietnam did not respond at that time, presumably out of a desire to maintain its independence of action and maximize its chances of obtaining aid from the West. By mid-1978, however, Hanoi's choices had narrowed. Not only were ties with China strained, but cautious efforts by the SRV to revitalize the negotiations with the United States (by suggesting that Hanoi might be willing to drop its demand for reconstruction assistance as a pre-condition for diplomatic ties) had so far elicited little response from Washington. The Carter Administration, beset with foreign policy problems of its own, now seemed in no hurry to seek a rapprochement with Vietnam.

The failure to improve relations with Washington and the increasing likelihood of a total aid cutoff from China apparently persuaded Hanoi to accept the earlier Soviet offer and request membership in CEMA. The formal decision took place at a meeting of the organization held in Bucharest in late June of 1978. While it was announced that the decision was unanimous, there were reports of unhappiness by several Eastern European members on the basis that the inclusion of Vietnam would represent a severe drain on the finances of the organization.

Some observers were skeptical of the benefits of membership in CEMA to the Vietnamese. While it would serve to integrate the Vietnamese economy into the planning and trade structure of the Soviet Union and its Eastern European allies, it would not substantially change the basic pattern of Vietnamese trade, the bulk of which was already with the socialist countries. On the other hand, it would provide access to needed raw materials, and preferential rates for Vietnamese exports, notably anthracite coal. More-over, there were soon indications that CEMA would be expected to take up some of the slack left by the cancellation of Chinese economic assistance. Shortly after the signing (and the final aid cutoff by Peking in early July) it was announced that the organization had agreed to support ten of the 80 projects dropped by Peking. Later a second announcement declared that a committee had been set up to study which additional projects were viable.[79]

Criticism of the Vietnamese decision to join CEMA was soon forthcoming from China and may have been the specific cause of the total aid cutoff. Hanoi defended its action by saying that it had been necessitated by Peking's cancellation of several projects in May. In the words of SRV Secretary of State Nguyen Co Thach: "without the cutting off of aid, this would not have been necessary. We entered Comecon (CEMA) only to find assistance."

The decision had obvious political implications, and Vietnamese sources admitted that the SRV would now be following a policy of "lean to one side" in the Sino-Soviet dispute. They insisted, however, that Vietnam remained independent and would not follow either the Soviet or the Chinese model.[80]

The pattern of closer relations with Moscow had repercussions in the military field. In the immediate aftermath of the war, Soviet military assistance (estimated at U.S. $255 million in 1975) had declined, but there were unconfirmed reports, denied by the Vietnamese, that the Soviet Union had requested use of the naval facilities at Da Nang and the old American base at Cam Ranh Bay further down the coast. Then, in March, 1978, three Soviet warships, including a guided missile cruiser, a frigate, and a minesweeper, arrived at Cam Ranh Bay for a brief visit. Later in the spring, Western intelligence sources noted the presence in Vietnam of two Soviet TU-95D reconnaissance planes, and the rumors began again. Foreign military specialists stated that access to the facilities at Cam Ranh Bay and Da Nang would represent a major military breakthrough for the Soviet Union, whose only major naval base in the Far East was at Vladivostok. Cam Ranh Bay in particular was well equipped to handle the Soviet Far Eastern Fleet, now at 12 warships, since it possessed substantial docking and overhaul facilities and an airstrip suitable for large combat aircraft. Hanoi continued to deny that the Soviet Union had been granted permanent facilities and said that brief stopovers by Soviet ships were just "normal practice."

Then, in early November, came a surprise announcement of the signing of a Treaty of Friendship and Cooperation with the Soviet Union. The treaty, scheduled to run for 25 years with a twelve-month cancellation clause, called for cooperation in case of a military attack on either party, but did not require specific action. The key passage read:

> In case either party is attacked or threatened with attack, the two parties signatory to the Treaty shall immediately consult with each other with a view to eliminating that threat and shall take appropriate and effective measures to safeguard peace and the security of the two countries.[81]

To many of Hanoi's neighbors, the signing of the treaty seemed additional evidence that Vietnam had sold its independence and become Moscow's proxy in Southeast Asia. Vietnamese sources retorted that the provisions in the treaty were not unique, and indeed were similar in most respects to those that the Soviet Union had signed with such neutral countries as Iraq and India. To the contrary, as one official noted, the treaty would give Vietnam "a greater margin to maneuver to develop its policy of independence," and demonstrate to anyone who wants to take measures against "little Vietnam" that it would have to consider the consequences.[82]

Hanoi's insistence that the treaty did not necessarily make Vietnam a puppet of the Soviet Union has some merit. Its provisions do not inherently infringe the SRV's freedom of action in international affairs. What was most noteworthy was that it aligned Hanoi firmly with Moscow in its dispute with Peking, a step which the Vietnamese had successfully been able to avoid during thirty years of war. And the scope of the decision was such that it virtually guaranteed Chinese animosity to Vietnam for the foreseeable future. For its part, Peking must assume that the treaty was directed primarily against China.   That assumption appeared confirmed a few months later when Secretary of State Nguyen Co Thach remarked that the treaty was signed only after China began to concentrate military forces on the Vietnamese border and made obvious preparations for an invasion.[83]

China's growing irritation at the intimacy of Vietnam-Soviet relations exerted a perceptible ripple effect on other issues of mutual importance between Hanoi and Peking. In the late 1970s, one of the most visible of these issues dealt with conflicting territorial claims. Recent statements on both sides make it clear that territorial disagreements had existed long before the end of the Vietnam conflict but had been papered over in the interests of maintaining a solid front in the war effort. At the close of the war, however, Sino-Vietnamese relations deteriorated rapidly and as the smoldering historical antagonism between the two countries began to flare up, the territorial conflict once again assumed major importance.

As in the case of Cambodia, the sources of disagreement were primarily located in three areas: 1) the land border, 2) a series of offshore islands claimed by both, and 3) the demarcation of the territorial seabed. Again, as with the case of Cambodia, the disagreement over the land border was relatively minor, but nonetheless led to armed conflict. The frontier had originally been delineated shortly after the French conquest of Tonkin in the mid-1880s. In two treaties signed between France and the Ch'ing Dynasty in 1887 and 1895 an agreement was reached on a common border, and boundary markers were laid out. In outward appearance that settlement was satisfactory to both parties and no major disturbances took place while the French retained their presence in Indochina. Even after the communist takeover in mainland China and North Vietnam, the border question did not immediately become a major issue in government-to-government relations. Recent evidence shows, however, that minor disputes over the land border did exist and discussions between local representatives of both countries took place in the autumn of 1956. These talks were apparently unsuccessful, and the following year the issue was referred to the central governments. At that time the Secretariat of the VWP Central Committee proposed that for the time being the status quo be maintained and that any disagreements should be settled through peaceful negotiations at the central governmental level. In a reply dated April, 1958, Peking agreed.[84]

In 1974 negotiations resumed. At that time it became apparent that although the differences were minor in their geographical scope, they were substantial in terms of their political implications. Both sides expressed a willingness to base a settlement on the existing border originally defined in 1887 and 1895 and confirmed as the status quo in the exchange of letters in 1957 and 1958. But each claimed that in certain instances the local authorities and inhabitants on the other side had seized territory, moved border markers, and made illegal settlements on lands possessed by the other. According to one Chinese source, the total area under contention was less than 60 kilometers. Yet many of the areas subject to disagreement are apparently of considerable economic importance to the local inhabitants. Some reflect ownership of roads or rail lines, of waterways or irrigation works, or access to pastureland or natural resources. The problem is complicated by the fact that most of the local residents in the areas under contention are ethnically related to the population on the other side of the border, and some sources have suggested that Hanoi is concerned that the Chinese are attempting to subvert the minority population on the Vietnamese side of the border.[85]

By the mid-1970s the tension had begun to break out in sporadic cases of armed violence along the border. There were persistent claims on both sides of harassment, seizure of territory, unilateral displacement or destruction of border markers, and even the kidnapping or killing of local citizens. According to sources on both sides, by 1978 several thousand incidents of provocations had been recorded, and both sides had lodged protests against the activities of the other.

A second source of dispute related to the demarcation of the territorial seabed in the Gulf of Tonkin. Article II of the 1887 Convention between China and France had stipulated that the offshore boundary along the northeastern frontier should be set at 108 degrees, 03 minutes, and 18 seconds (Greenwich). At that time, however, offshore territorial boundaries were limited to three miles and the concept of a territorial sea had not yet arisen, so the delineation of the offshore boundary had been solely for the purpose of establishing ownership over the offshore islands near the coast.

For decades, there were no problems between the two countries over the Gulf, and Peking claims it even ceded several small islands inhabited by Chinese to the DRV. Then, in December, 1973, Hanoi informed Peking of its intention to sign contracts with foreign concerns to prospect for oil in the Gulf of Tonkin and proposed negotiations to delineate the territorial sea in the area. China accepted the proposal to open negotiations but insisted that enterprises of third countries should not be permitted to participate in the exploitation of the resources in the Gulf of Tonkin, and that no prospecting should take place in the rectangle bounded by the 18th to the 20th parallels and the 107th to the 108th meridians, an area likely to be under dispute in negotiations. Hanoi agreed, and talks on delineation of the Gulf opened in August, 1974, in Peking.

As with the dispute over the land border, the negotiations immediately ran into snags. Vietnam suggested that the line established by the 1887 Convention be accepted as the basis for determining the boundary for the division of the territorial sea in the Gulf. Peking declined, pointing out that the division of territorial waters in the Gulf of Tonkin could not have been the original intent of the Sino-French agreement since it related solely to the purpose of determining ownership over the offshore islands close to the mainland. Acceptance of the Vietnamese claim, moreover, would give the Vietnamese two-thirds of the Gulf. Negotiations resumed in 1977, but agreement remained elusive. For the time being, an arrangement was reached that the area in the middle of the Gulf be declared closed to exploitation until the two parties could reach agreement. Recently, however, this too has come into question as Peking has signed a contract with an American oil consortium to conduct offshore seismic surveys in the Gulf. While these are exploratory only, and the bulk of the concession is located on the Chinese side of the median between Vietnam and Hainan Island, a portion of the concession area reportedly falls into the zone declared off-limits. In the meantime, Vietnam has awarded similar contracts to several European companies, and parts of the concession fall within areas claimed by China.[86]

One final source of disagreement is somewhat more complicated and may be the most difficult to resolve. The issue revolves around two small collections of islands, some no more than coral reefs, in the South China Sea: the Paracels (directly west of the coast of Central Vietnam) and the Spratlys (a more diverse group spread out between Vietnam and the Philippine island of Palawan). The problem is complicated by history. Both island groups are currently claimed by Hanoi and Peking. The later is claimed by Manila as well. Historical documents in the possession of the PRC indicate that both island groups were discovered, claimed, and occasionally occupied by the Chinese Empire as early as the period of the Three Kingdoms in the early Christian era. Chinese occupation, however, was apparently intermittent, and did not continue in an uninterrupted fashion down to the present century. The advent of colonialism predictably changed the scope of the situation. Until the 1930s, France apparently did not formally contest Chinese sovereignty over the islands. In 1921 French foreign minister Aristide Briand conceded that since 1909 China had exercised sovereignty - in an apparent reference to a naval inspection visit paid by a Chinese fleet to the Paracels in 1909. The discovery of the presence of guano - an important source for the manufacture of artificial fertilizer - on the Paracels brought economic issues into play, however, and in 1931 France seized the islands, contending that the Empire of Annam had "prior title" to the Paracels. This claim was rejected by the Nanking Republic but, lacking the power to contest the seizure, it took no action.[87] During the Pacific War both island groups were occupied by Japan, but at the close of the war, competition resumed. The Paracels were briefly occupied by the Republic of China, and then, in August 1951, by the new communist government in Peking, which declared the Paracels historically Chinese. During succeeding years, the PRC controlled most of the islands and undertook a program to settle them, mostly by Hainanese, while a small military base was constructed on Yung Xing island. In the early 1960s, the Saigon regime briefly settled a few of the unoccupied islands, but in January 1974 a Chinese naval force drove them out.

The case of the Spratlys was equally complex. More isolated and spread out, and of less apparent economic value than the Paracels, they were rarely occupied during the premodern period. Since 1946, the Republic of China has occupied Itu Aba, one of the major islands of the group. In 1956, the Saigon regime seized three islands which had been occupied by the French before World War II and took several more after the loss of the Paracels to China in 1974. Finally, in 1971 the Philippines laid claim to the islands on the basis of their proximity to the island of Palawan, and landed 1,000 soldiers on the island of Pagasa, where it plans to construct a marina and a fishing port.

The communist regime in Hanoi has only recently become actively involved in the controversy over ownership of the two island groups. Preoccupied with the war effort in South Vietnam and undoubtedly anxious to avoid provoking Peking, the DRV made no specific claims to either island group before 1974.

Its only specific official reference to the question came in September, 1958, when Prime Minister Pham Van Dong, in response to a letter from his Chinese counterpart Chou En-lai written a few days earlier, declared that the DRV recognized and supported the declaration of the PRC on Chinese territorial waters. Chou's original note had stated that China's territorial sea was twelve nautical miles and included the Xisha and the Nansha Islands (the Chinese names for the Paracels and the Spratlys). Dong's reply was somewhat ambiguous and simply referred to China's declaration of a twelve-mile territorial sea.

After the close of the war, Hanoi changed its attitude. In the spring of 1975 units of the PAVN seized the six islands of the Spratlys previously occupied by the Saigon regime. Then, in May of 1977, the Vietnamese military newspaper Quan Doi Nhan Dan published a map marking both island groups as Vietnamese territory. At the same time the regime laid its claim for a 200 mile territorial sea. China has reacted to these events with outrage. It contends that Pham Van Dong's letter of September, 1958, serves as formal Vietnamese recognition of China's ownership over both island groups, and claims that the Vietnamese government has now gone back on their word. Peking cites as further evidence the fact that atlases published in the DRV in later years called the islands by their Chinese names and labelled them as Chinese. Hanoi, however, has not backed down. In August, 1979, it asserted that "the spirit and letter" of Pham Van Dong's note "were confined to recognition of China's twelve-mile territorial waters." One month later, it presented several historical documents to support its claim that the Paracels and the Spratlys, called in Vietnamese the Hoang Sa and the Truong Sa respectively had been originally discovered and administered by the Vietnamese Empire.[88]

To this date, there has been no settlement of the issue. In 1978, during a visit to Manila by Foreign Minister Nguyen Duy Trinh, Vietnam and the Phillipines agreed in a joint statement to discuss their conflicting claims over the Spratlys in a spirit of friendship. Hanoi attempted to strengthen its own hand by accepting Philippine jurisdiction over five of the Spratlys in return for Manila's recognition of Vietnamese ownership over three others. China and Vietnam, however, have been unable to resolve their own differences. Hanoi sent Deputy Foreign Minister Phan Hien to Peking in 1978 in an effort to promote talks, but China refused to negotiate, claiming there was nothing to discuss. Vietnam refuses to accept Peking's contention that it has already recognized Chinese sovereignty over the islands. In this perspective, it seems likely that the ambiguity in Pham Van Dong's 1958 letter was deliberate. Since Hanoi undoubtedly did not wish to antagonize China in time of war it took refuge in diplomatic doubletalk.[89] The problem is now complicated by the fact that recent exploratory efforts have suggested the presence of substantial oil reserves in the general area northwest of Palawan Island. If so, the significance of the area to all contestants will be measurably increased and the differences correspondingly more difficult to resolve.

The Third Indochina War

By the end of 1977, tension between Vietnam and Cambodia had grown intense. Since early in the year, Pol Pot had been conducting a purge of all pro-Hanoi elements in his government, Party, and armed forces and, according to one report, had eliminated several regional and divisional commanders, political commissars, and five out of twenty members of the KCP Central Committee. During September and October, Cambodian troops continued their incursions into Vietnamese territory between Ha Tien and Chau Doc, and in some cases penetrated up to four miles beyond the border, destroying combat hamlets and NEAs and massacring the local inhabitants.

In the first week of December, Vietnamese troops launched a counterattack which penetrated up to 35 miles into Cambodia, chiefly in the area of the Parrot's Beak, directly west of Ho Chi Minh City. Then they began to withdraw, while Hanoi proposed negotiations and formally denied any intention of forming an Indochinese Federation. In February, the SRV presented a three-point proposal calling for negotiations, a cease-fire line five kilometers from the border, and a territorial settlement based on the pre-1954 line drawn by the French. Cambodia rejected the proposal, however, and continued to wage harassing attacks along the border. Apparently Hanoi's decision to attack Cambodia was taken at a meeting of the Central Committee sometime early in 1978, in response to Phnom Penh's refusal to discuss a peaceful settlement. According to rumors, there may have been some disagreement over the means to be used. According to one report, Soviet leaders suggested a quick surgical strike similar to their own invasion of Czechoslovakia in 1968. The Vietnamese preferred to do it their own way and settled on the familiar combination of a general offensive led by regular forces combined with a popular uprising involving Cambodian guerillas trained in Vietnam and local demonstrations by the masses. This pattern of attack had been adopted by Hanoi during the final stages of the war against South Vietnam. If the Cambodian invasion followed that precedent, however, the primary burden of the attack would be borne by regular force units of the PAVN.

Of Hanoi's overall military superiority over the forces of Democratic Kampuchea there was no doubt. With a total of over 600,000 in its armed forces (about a third of which were in South Vietnam) paramilitary forces of 70,000, and a local self-defense militia of well over a million, the Vietnamese army was one of the strongest in Asia. It was well equipped with Soviet and American tanks, personnel carriers, artillery, and combat aircraft. By contrast, the Cambodian army numbered less than 200,000. Although it was receiving some assistance from China, it was poorly equipped, relatively inexperienced, and the loyalty of several of its military commanders (as a series of mutinies along the eastern border had demonstrated) was seriously in doubt.

Hanoi's major military problem, then, was not in sheer numbers, or in firepower. It was in morale. In operations along the border in 1977, Vietnamese troops reportedly had performed poorly. Sources in Hanoi attributed much of the problem to lack of discipline and low morale. A conference sponsored by the Central Military Party Committee on discipline in the armed forces concluded that some commanders had failed to take charge of the situation within their own combat units. According to a directive issued at the conference:

> The undisciplined situation in the lower level in some
> divisions and regiments has been prolonged and comes to
> the cadres' attention only when it becomes severe.[90]

The causes of the problem were not always immediately apparent. In part, they may have reflected a rise in war-weariness that is understandable after two decades of bitter fighting. Then, too, Hanoi press reports admitted that there were distressing signs of corruption and laxity within many military units. Some observed that the bulk of the problem came from units composed of native South Vietnamese. Whatever the reasons, the Party's military leadership responded with a campaign to stamp out corruption and indiscipline in the armed forces. A number of high-level military officers considered responsible for the problem were replaced. Several younger officers who had performed aggressively and well during the final campaign against the Saigon regime were placed in positions of command responsibility.[91]

By mid-summer, the effort to strengthen military preparedness had intensified. All existing military units were placed on nationwide alert, and many soldiers demobilized after the fall of Saigon were called back into the service. Conscription of all able-bodied males of 18 to 25 years of age was ordered, and women of 18 to 20 were encouraged to join on a volunteer basis. For the purposes of strengthening local defense, each of Vietnam's 500 districts was instructed to recruit a division of self-defense militia at the village level, and to "transform each district into a military fortress." At the same time, controls were tightened throughout society as a whole. Population "nests" of thirty to fifty families each were reportedly formed among the civilian population, with each nest selecting a security chief and a police officer. All overnight absences by local residents from the area were to be reported, and all visitors were required to register with the security officer.[92]

Along the Cambodian border, clashes continued throughout the summer of 1978. At one point in June, Cambodian ground units, reportedly supported by Chinese tanks and heavy artillery, penetrated nearly 10 miles into Vietnamese territory. The heaviest fighting took place along the north edge of the Parrot's Beak. By the end of September, there was fighting all along the border and several Cambodian towns, including Mimot and Krek, had been placed under siege by the PAVN. In the meantime, a progressive buildup of Vietnamese forces along the border took place in preparation for an invasion to be launched with the onset of the winter dry season. A guerilla force of 25,000 had been recruited out of the 150,000 Khmer refugees in South Vietnam. The leader was reported to be So Phim, a former secretary of a KCP regional party committee who had defected when suspected of disloyalty by the Pol Pot government.

In early December, a new anti-Pol Pot liberation front, called the National United Front for the National Salvation of Kampuchea (KNUFNS), was set up somewhere in a liberated area in Eastern Cambodia. The leader of the new front was Heng Samrin, a virtually unknown former division commander of Pol Pot's forces who had defected to the Vietnamese in April 1978. The new front proclaimed an eleven-point program calling for the restoration of freedom of residence, movement, association and religion, promised an end to forced labor and pay according to work (rather than the existing utopian prescription of pay according to need), and a planned economy with markets, banks, and a national currency. In Hanoi, the formation of KNUFNS was described as a "major turning point" in the Cambodian civil conflict.[93]

By the middle of December, Hanoi had massed 135,000 troops near the border and had thrust through the Parrot's Beak and the Fishhook (slightly to the north) to within 25 miles of Kratie. On the 25th, PAVN units totalling over 100,000 troops and supported by airpower and Cambodian guerrillas moved in force deeper into Cambodian territory. The main initial route of advance was toward the northwest. In five days the invading forces had seized Kratie, on the main branch of the Mekong River. Then they headed southwest down the river toward Kompong Cham and cut the route to Phnom Penh. In the meantime a new front opened in the south as additional Vietnamese units attacked across the border to seize Takeo and then moved directly north toward the capital, with motorized units advancing along the major highways supported by air cover.

Hanoi's strategy was evidently a surprise to the Cambodians, who had placed the bulk of their force near the Parrot's Beak on the assumption that the Vietnamese would invade directly up Route 7 as they had the previous year. Now they were outflanked by the two-pronged Vietnamese offensive. Harassed by aerial bombing and decimated by heavy ground assaults (the Vietnamese units were reportedly using the familiar "blooming lotus" technique, involving direct attacks on the heart of the enemy's formation and then branching out to mop up resistance), the Cambodian army began to break. As diplomats and Chinese workers fled the capital, the Pol Pot government and its military headquarters retreated to the mountains along the coast, where they set up a new command post and attempted to regroup. On January 7th, Phnom Penh was taken.

On January 8th, the new government was installed in Phnom Penh. Heng Samrin was announced as president of an eight-man People's Revolutionary Council. The Vietnamese representative at the United Nations called for recognition of the new Democratic People's Republic of Kampuchea (DPRK) as the legitimate government of Cambodia. On February 18th, a Treaty of Peace, Friendship and Cooperation was signed with the SRV in Phnom Penh. In the meantime, Vietnamese units continued their advance toward the Thai border in an effort to mop up resistance from the remaining forces loyal to Pol Pot. Advancing along Routes 5 and 6, to the South and North of the Tonle Sap, they reached Sisophon in a few days and they cut off 10,000 Cambodian troops located at Battambang. Additional troops were sent to the Thai border at Poipet and Pailin and to the Cardamom Mountains to cut off escape and prevent Khmer Rouge forces from consolidating their position along the coast.

The Cambodian Invasion and Regional Politics

The Vietnamese invasion of Cambodia presented other nations in the area with a dilemma. Few had much sympathy for the brutal regime of Pol Pot which, according to reliable reports, had been responsible for the deaths of millions of Cambodians. Yet the Vietnamese invasion of Cambodia could hardly be described as other than a blatant act of interference in the internal affairs of a sovereign nation. While Hanoi's description of the invasion as a popular uprising may not have been without some foundation (the evidence does suggest that the defeat of

Pol Pot was greeted with considerable enthusiasm in much of the country), the massive presence of the PAVN - in light of historic Cambodian distrust of the Vietnamese - was not likely to be popular. And Hanoi's action was a vivid demonstration of Hanoi's willingness to use force as an instrument in its foreign policy.

Unquestionably, outside of the Pol Pot regime itself, the biggest loser in the war was China. Although obviously viewing the radical policies of its client regime with distaste, Peking had increasingly been impelled to rely on the new revolutionary Cambodia as a bulwark against Vietnamese and Soviet expansion in Southeast Asia. In 1977 and 1978 it provided military assistance and several thousand Chinese advisers to the Phnom Penh government. Initially it attempted to avoid becoming embroiled in the conflict with Vietnam and may have hoped to play the role of mediator. As the conflict grew more intense, however, Peking was increasingly drawn to the side of Phnom Penh in its struggle against what the PRC called "the forces of Soviet Social imperialism." In July of 1978 one high Chinese official remarked that China could not watch with indifference any infringement on Cambodian sovereignty and would support Cambodia and her people in their struggle.[94]

Yet China was in a poor position to provide direct assistance to the Pol Pot regime in its hour of desperation. When Foreign Minister Ieng Sary went to Peking following the invasion in an effort to obtain military support, the Chinese government made it clear that it would not become directly involved in the conflict and advised the Cambodians to prepare to wage a protracted struggle against the Vietnam-supported regime in Phnom Penh. To reduce the odious reputation the Pol Pot government had earned in the international arena, Ieng Sary was advised to form a broad national front with all anti-Vietnamese and anti-communist forces operating in Cambodia.

If the invasion of Cambodia heightened the tension between Hanoi and Peking, it also represented a major setback to hopes for an improvement in Vietnamese relations with the ASEAN states. Immediately prior to the beginning of the Cambodian invasion in December, the Vietnamese regime had launched a diplomatic offensive. In an extended tour of ASEAN capitals, Foreign Minister Nguyen Duy Trinh had stressed Hanoi's desire for amicable relations with its neighbors. Deputy Foreign Minister Phan Hien, while in Kuala Lumpur, suggested that Vietnam was now ready to discuss the original ASEAN proposal for a regional zone of peace, rather than its own. In talks held in Bangkok, Pham Van Dong offered a non-aggression and anti-subversion clause in a draft proposal for a treaty of friendship and cooperation with Thailand.[95] In a previous visit, Dong and Thai Prime Minister Kriangsak Chamanand had expressed determination to refrain from subversion, direct or indirect, against each other or to threaten each other with force. While the Thai government expressed no interest in a formal treaty, the two parties did reach agreement on a joint communique calling for "the desirability of Southeast Asia as an area of peace, independence, freedom and neutrality."

The Vietnamese invasion of Cambodia dealt a severe blow to the delicate web of Vietnamese contacts with the ASEAN states, who suspected that Hanoi's peace offensive the previous fall had been a ruse to mislead Vietnam's neighbors as to her real intentions. The presence of Vietnamese military units along the Thai border, and the obvious intention of the Khmer Rouge to use Thai territory as a sanctuary for further operations in Cambodia, raised the specter of a wider war and a possible Vietnamese invasion of Thailand. The ASEAN states reacted to the offensive with a quick gesture of solidarity, and in mid-January issued a joint statement indirectly censuring Vietnam and calling for the withdrawal of all foreign troops from Cambodia. All but the Philippines offered aid to Thailand if the latter were subjected to attack. But the prospect was an alarming one. Vietnamese military forces were equal in size to those of all of ASEAN, and undeniably superior in quality and experience.

Undoubtedly of greater concern was the effect of the war on relations with the United States. During the late summer and early fall of 1978, prospects for normalization had appeared to improve when Hanoi formally dropped its demand for the reconstruction assistance promised by ex-President Nixon in 1973. By September the two sides were close to agreement. But as so often had been the case, the course of events bedeviled the efforts of Hanoi and Washington to come to a meeting of minds. Increased tension along the Cambodian border, the unsavory image of the Hanoi regime driving out the "boat people," and then in November the news of the signing of the Treaty with Moscow, caused the Carter Administration to back away. In December, Washington warned that increased Vietnamese involvement in Cambodia would set back diplomatic relations. The invasion, coupled with the Sino-Vietnamese War, wrote at least a temporary halt to American interest in improving relations with Hanoi. The United States did not wish to jeopardize prospects for a rapprochement with Peking at a time when a breakthrough was immanent. To put it bluntly, the Carter Administration felt that it had little to gain in normalizing ties with Vietnam. It had a good deal to lose.[96]

War with China

While problems in relations with ASEAN and the United States were probably viewed as unfortunate consequences of the Cambodian invasion, they were evidently considered acceptable. ASEAN clearly did not represent a military threat to Vietnam. Moreover, the political views of the ASEAN states were too diverse to permit the alliance to present a united front on the issue for an extended period of time. To put it frankly, the damage could be undone later. As for normalization of relations with the United States, that too was an issue that could await its time. With massive economic assistance not a likely by-product of normalization, the importance of friendly relations with Washington may have declined in Hanoi, and certainly did not match the importance of close links with Moscow and Phnom Penh.

The most dangerous potential consequence of the Cambodian invasion was the reaction of Peking. The overthrow of the Pol Pot regime was a direct affront to China, and while its leaders had been cautious in their statements during the crisis, top officials in Peking had noted ominously that China could not tolerate with indifference any open infringement of the territorial sovereignty of its ally in Phnom Penh. During his visit to the United States during the height of the crisis, PRC Deputy Prime Minister Teng Hsiao-p'ing spoke pointedly of the need to administer a lesson to the "small hegemonist" in Hanoi.

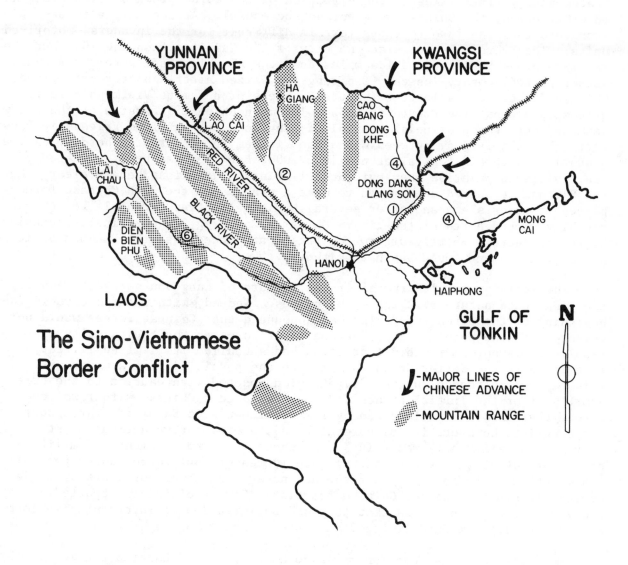

The Sino-Vietnamese
Border Conflict

China apparently gave final approval to the decision to attack Vietnam
during a plenary session of the CCP Central Committee held in December.[97] It
seems likely that serious consideration had been given prior to that, however,
since China had been concentrating military forces along the Vietnamese border
since the previous fall. The invasion was launched on February 17th. The
attacking force numbered over 80,000, with additional units totalling over
120,000 maintained in reserve. The invaders concentrated on five main objectives - the border capitals of Lang Son, Lao Cai, Lai Chau, Ha Giang and Cao
Bang. Although there were a few setpiece battles, for the most part the PLA
did not use the technique of direct assault, but began by infiltrating small
assault squads around Vietnamese positions to undermine them; then main force
units would advance down the highways, burning the forest cover, blowing up
tunnels and destroying Vietnamese defensive installations. The deepest penetra-
tion took place in the West, where Chinese units took Lai Chau and then pene-

trated nearly fifty miles in the direction of the border town of Dien Bien Phu. In other areas, the Chinese were not so successful. At Lao Cai, a three-pronged attack ran into tortuous terrain difficult for the invaders' motorized units. They were able to seize the city of Lao Cai itself on the 19th but then ran into heavy resistance a few miles down the Red River and were thrown back with reportedly heavy losses. Cao Bang was seized after a bitter battle and Chinese forces were able to cut Route 4, scene of a famous Vietminh border offensive against the French in 1950. The main Chinese offensive of the war was launched near the provincial capital of Lang Son, not far from Friendship Pass, where the main railway between China and Vietnam intersects the border. Normally a bustling mountain capital of nearly 50,000, Lang Son had been evacuated of its civilian population when evidence of Chinese intentions became clear. Here the Vietnamese seemed determined to make a stand. On the 27th Chinese forces placed it under siege and after several bruising battles were able to seize the high ground north of the city. On March 2nd Lang Son was finally occupied by the invaders. Shortly afterward, Peking announced that the PLA had achieved its objectives and would begin to withdraw.[98]

The decision to withdraw after the seizure of Lang Son served to confirm the restricted nature of China's objectives. Indeed, within a few days of the beginning of the offensive Peking had announced that Chinese forces would not advance into the populous Red River Delta or threaten the capital city of Hanoi. It is not improbable that China had signalled its limited military intentions to the Soviet Union to minimize the possibility of a wider war. This may be one reason why the Soviet Union reacted with caution to the crisis. Shortly after the initial attacks, Moscow demanded a Chinese withdrawal and warned that the USSR would stand by its commitments to Hanoi.[99] Throughout the conflict, however, it was careful to avoid provocative actions or statements. Leaves for army reservists were cancelled, and shipments of military equipment (by airlift via Calcutta) were increased, but there was no general mobilization of Soviet armed forces, and no evident troop movements by the 44 Soviet divisions along the Chinese frontier. Soviet officials reportedly assured diplomats in Moscow that they had no intention of intervening so long as the conflict remained limited.

Moscow's cautious reaction may also have reflected Hanoi's confidence that it could handle the crisis without active involvement by Russian forces. In fact, informed observers concluded that the Vietnamese performed well. Although outnumbered nearly two to one in the immediate area of the frontier, and compelled to resist Chinese main force units with border troops or regional forces, the Vietnamese defenders imposed severe losses on the attackers. As might be expected, casualty figures varied according to the source, but most impartial estimates seem to place losses at nearly 50,000 for each side. There was a moment, at the fall of Lang Son in early March, when the Hanoi regime briefly appeared ready to call up one or more of its main force divisions stationed near the capital, and there were reports that some units in Laos were shifted to North Vietnam. But on the whole, Hanoi did not panic. The defenders performed credibly, and demonstrated convincingly that their victory in the war in South Vietnam had been no fluke. In particular, the local forces near the border played a major role in blunting the force of the Chinese invasion, and justified the confidence of the Party's military strategists in the validity of the concept of people's war as an integral component in national defense.

On the Chinese side, the government announced that it had succeeded in its objective of "exploding the myth of the invincibility of the 'Asian Cuba'." Indeed, in two weeks of fighting the PLA had managed to seize several provincial capitals and impose severe casualties on the defenders. According to outside military observers, Chinese units had fought bravely and well. On the other hand, the PLA had shown some serious logistical weaknesses, as well as a shortage of modern equipment. Coordination between ground troops, artillery, and tanks was haphazard, a problem that would not seen to be unusual for a military force that had not been involved in heavy fighting for over two decades.[100] The war showed the Chinese leadership that military modernization must necessarily become a matter of high national priority for the foreseeable future.

As Chinese forces began to withdraw in mid-March, Peking offered negotiations. At first Hanoi refused on the grounds that foreign troops were "still trampling on our soil," and later because PLA units continued to occupy territories along the border even after the withdrawal was completed. Eventually, however, Hanoi agreed to a Chinese proposal to hold negotiations at the deputy foreign minister level alternatively in Hanoi and Peking. In mid-April a Chinese delegation under Deputy Foreign Minister Han Nien-long arrived in Hanoi and peace talks commenced. The Chinese immediately presented an eight-point proposal, the main provisions of which called for mutual opposition to hegemonism (an obvious reference to the Soviet Union) and to the stationing of troops in foreign countries (an equally obvious reference to the Vietnamese forces in Cambodia), acceptance of the Sino-French boundary agreement as the basis for a negotiated settlement of the land border, mutual respect for the concept of the twelve mile territorial sea, Vietnamese recognition of Chinese ownership of the Paracel and Spratly Islands, mutual respect for the rights, interests, and personal safety of nations of the other country, and permission for Chinese refugees in China to return to Vietnam. The Vietnamese delegation rejected the Chinese proposal and offered one of its own, providing for a cease-fire and mutual release of prisoners, restoration of normal relations, and a settlement of the territorial dispute on the basis of the accords of 1887 and 1895.[101]

The nature of the negotiating positions taken by the two sides indicated that for the moment, neither was ready to consider resolution of the outstanding issues in their mutual relations. Indeed, after several sessions held in Hanoi and Peking over the year, no visible progress had been achieved and in March of 1980 Peking suggested that the talks be adjourned until a more favorable time. In the meantime clashes along the land border have continued and Hanoi has charged that China is preparing to launch a new invasion. Peking has not ruled out "teaching Vietnam another lesson," but there has been no evidence of a troop buildup along the frontier similar to the one which took place prior to the 1979 war. Indeed it would be difficult to repeat even the limited success achieved with the previous invasion. The element of surprise would be lacking (Hanoi has admitted that it was not totally prepared for the scope and direction of the initial attacks) and there are reliable reports that Vietnam has substantially strengthened its forces along the frontier.[102]

Building the New Cambodia

If one of the objectives of the Chinese invasion of Vietnam had been to weaken Hanoi's position in Cambodia, or to persuade it to change its policy there, it was not effective. Vietnamese military units were not transferred to the front in North Vietnam and continued their mopping up operations against the scattered resistance forces of Pol Pot, while Vietnamese advisers assisted the new DPRK as it moved to consolidate its rule in Phnom Penh. Gradually the excesses of the previous regime were eliminated and the imprint of communism Vietnamese-style began to make its mark. The radical policies of the previous regime - the elimination of all forms of religion and traditional family life, the evacuation of the cities and the herding of virtually the entire population into vast work camps, and the executions of all those suspected of sympathy with the past regime - were reversed, and new moderate policies were put into effect. Rural communes were replaced by small-scale cooperatives, the practice of religion was once again permitted, markets were opened and a new national currency established, and gradually the population began to return to the cities. To provide itself with the cloak of legitimacy, the new government promised to write a new constitution and hold elections for a new national assembly. The essential mark of a communist regime was retained, however. The KCP, carefully purged of Pol Pot supporters, retained its dominant political role in society under the familiar Dictatorship of the Proletariat.

The new regime had relatively little trouble in re-establishing security throughout much of the country. DPRK Foreign Minister Hun Sen claimed to a foreign journalist that the Khmer Rouge could be defeated in two months if the sanctuaries in Thailand could be cleaned out. But if it was one thing to put an end to organized military resistance, it was quite another to provide the new government with an image of legitimacy, a dedicated and experienced bureaucracy, and a base of support among the mass of the population. Throughout the remainder of the year few nations outside the socialist bloc granted diplomatic recognition to the new regime and in November the UN General Assembly demanded the withdrawal of Vietnamese occupation forces. The government itself found it difficult to recruit competent cadres. Virtually the entire educated class of Cambodia had been executed by the previous regime or fled to other countries. The new government, inevitably identified with the hated Vietnamese occupation forces, found it difficult to establish a popular base in society. Worst of all, the country was woefully short of food, and the continuing anarchy in rural areas created the possibility of mass starvation in the countryside. Promises of grain shipments from foreign suppliers had only minimum effect as the regime was suspicious of outsiders, and encountered problems in distribution. Some critics charged that the Heng Samrin government deliberately withheld rice from the population, but while it is probably true that the urban population and the armed forces were provided with more generous rations, the problem was probably more a consequence of inefficiency than of willfull obstructionism. As one spokesman for the regime conceded, "technical and structural problems" were seriously hampering the effective administration of government.

The gradual if erratic consolidation of power by the Heng Samrin regime served to reduce the international outcry that had greeted the initial invasion in December, but did not entirely eliminate it. Although a few Western governments (notably Great Britain) decided to grant diplomatic recognition to the new regime,   many others, including the United States and the ASEAN states, did not and continued to press for a Vietnamese withdrawal and the formation of a broader government in Phnom Penh representing the diverse political factions in Cambodia. Hanoi ignored such appeals and called the occupation an "internal matter." It made no apology for its behavior. "Struggle," said one Vietnamese publication, "is a law of life."[103]

Throughout the spring and summer international efforts were undertaken to break the impasse. The most publicized proposal called for the return of Prince Sihanouk to head a government of all factions in a neutralist Cambodia. Since his overthrow in March of 1970 Sihanouk's political career had been in abeyance. After initially seeking refuge in Peking, he reluctantly accepted the titular leadership of the National Front led by Pol Pot's Khmer Rouge. After the rise to power of the latter in 1975 he returned to Cambodia where he provided an element of international respectability to the new revolutionary regime. The KCP leadership, however, made no secret of its distrust of the volatile and imperious prince and kept him in virtual house arrest. Finally he returned once more to Peking where he vociferously complained of the brutality of the Khmer Rouge regime. With the overthrow of Pol Pot his name was raised once again as a possible solution to the knotty Cambodian problem. Sihanouk appeared willing, and in June he proposed an international conference to discuss a solution to the Cambodian problem.

For a time there appeared a brief glimmer of hope for a compromise solution. There were persistent rumors that Hanoi, embarrassed by the damage to its international reputation and groaning under the cost of the Cambodian occupation, might be willing to accept Sihanouk as a way out of the impasse. Within weeks, however, the proposal was dead. In late summer, Hanoi declared publicly that the Prince would only be acceptable if he abandoned his ties with China, and if the KCP remained in firm control, for the trend in Cambodia "is inexorably toward socialism." In any case, Vietnamese sources added, Heng Samrin would have to give his approval to any such solution.[104] For China, which in any case had been a reluctant sponsor of the mercurial Prince who was so frequently critical of his hosts, Hanoi's conditions were clearly unacceptable. Peking rejected the idea of an international conference on Cambodia as wishful thinking, and the idea was dropped.

With the Sihanouk formula abandoned, China and other nations opposed to international recognition of the Heng Samrin regime were forced to fall back on Pol Pot or a broader alliance of anti-DPRK forces including the Khmer Rouge. During the winter, Peking attempted to encourage its ally to improve its image by forming a united front with other political factions like the pro-Western Khmer Serei, and apparently suggested that Pol Pot himself resign as head of the movement. When the change came, however, it was only cosmetic. In early 1980 Pol Pot stepped down as prime minister in favor of his subordinate Khieu Samphan, but he retained his position of commander in chief of the armed forces.

The ASEAN states, too, groped for a solution to the problem that did not involve accepting the status quo. They continued to recognize Democratic Kampuchea as the legitimate government of Cambodia despite their reservations about Pol Pot, and supported a resolution in the UN General Assembly in November calling for the withdrawal of foreign troops from Cambodia. That appeal was repeated in a joint statement with members of the European Economic Community the following March. Simultaneously, however, efforts were underway through diplomatic channels in a more conciliatory vein. Malaysian Foreign Minister Rithaudeen, visiting Hanoi in December, was authorized by the organization to appeal to the Vietnamese leaders to accept a neutralist solution in Cambodia, and to tell them that they were going about the containment of China in the wrong way.

The Vietnamese were not entirely unreceptive to the efforts of their neighbors. In October, on a visit to Bangkok, Nguyen Co Thach promised that Vietnamese forces would not enter Thailand (he did warn that if Thailand gave support to the Khmer Rouge the PAVN might have to undertake operations along the border). But Hanoi would not make any substantive concessions on the Cambodian issue and rejected ASEAN efforts as "crude interference" in Cambodia's internal affairs. It asserted that the ASEAN demand for a withdrawal of Vietnamese occupation forces "does not conform to reality," and that those forces would remain in Cambodia for so long as the threat to that nation's security from China and the United States remained.[105]

Hanoi's unwillingness to pursue a compromise solution in Cambodia may reflect a variety of factors. In the first place, it may reflect the under-lying suspicion of the Vietnamese Party leadership for the underlying motives of the other parties to the dispute, notably China, the ASEAN states, and the United States. The legacy of bitterness and distrust left by the Vietnamese revolution had been considerable, and Hanoi's leaders, steeled in toughness, have undoubtedly developed a "fortress mentality" which is fundamentally averse to weakness and compromise. A generation of struggle has taught the Party leadership that only rock-hard determination can triumph over hostile forces abroad and at home.

By contrast, the regime may be convinced that despite its current problems, the long-range trend in Cambodia is in its favor. The current wave of outrage to Vietnamese actions in the global arena will decline with time. The ASEAN states are nervous about Vietnam, but they are equally concerned at the long-term danger from China. Already fissures have begun to appear in the alliance over a proper response to the continuing Vietnamese presence in Phnom Penh. As for the situation within Cambodia, Vietnam can hardly be unaware of the historic animosity of the Khmer peoples to their neighbors to the east. While that animosity cannot be expected to disappear overnight, it can be handled with the aid of a sympathetic and firmly guided regime in Phnom Penh. In any case, Hanoi's leaders may reason that Cambodia is too crucial to the security of Vietnam to permit a compromise solution. Under such circumstances, it is better to pursue the situation to its logical and desired conclusion, whatever the costs. It is noteworthy that one high official in Hanoi implied that the situation might have turned out differently if the DRV had acted against the Pol Pot regime in 1970, when the latter's animosity toward Hanoi had already been demonstrated. "Perhaps," he concluded, "we are now paying for that mistake."[1]

For the moment, Hanoi continues to bear a high cost for that determination. While open resistance to the regime in Phnom Penh has declined in recent months, anti-government forces continue to be active in rural areas, and have forced the Vietnamese to maintain a substantial military presence, estimated at 200,000, in the country. At the moment of writing, Vietnamese troops have allegedly crossed the border into Thailand in an operation designed to clean out the rebel forces operating in the sanctuary across the frontier. Hanoi, while denying that its troops have transgressed the border, admits that its troops are operating along the border in response to the decision by refugee officials in the area to repatriate several thousand Cambodian refugees, many of whom are thought to be active supporters of the Khmer Rouge. But it has provoked a sharp retort from ASEAN and on the domestic scene, the Heng Samrin regime continues to be plagued by a lack of professional cadres and popular support, and many outside observers have predicted that without the presence of the PAVN, it could not survive in power. On the moral plane, the new government has yet to make substantial progress in resolving the food shortage, which continues into the new decade. Not only is the 1980 harvest likely to be totally inadequate to feed the needy, but the prospects for next year seem even worse. Seeds are short, and many peasants have abandoned their farmsteads for the precarious security of the refugee camps.

The Revolution in Crisis

In the classical sense, danger from abroad tends to unite people of a beleagured revolutionary society behind the leadership in a concerted effort to save the new order. Whether this pattern is occurring in Vietnam today is difficult to say with certainty. One Vietnamese official recently remarked that it had been much easier for the regime to mobilize the people against their traditional Chinese enemy to the North than it had been earlier against the Americans in the South. While that may be the case, there are numerous signs that Hanoi's foreign entanglements have complicated the internal situation and exacerbated the tensions within society, within the government, and even within the Party leadership itself.

The signs of that malaise are clearly visible. On the one hand, the flow of refugees out of the country reached a peak in 1979. Beginning in the spring, the outflow increased rapidly as the authorities, now apparently confirmed in their suspicion of the loyalty of their Chinese subjects, put more pressure on ethnic Chinese to emigrate or to move to NEAs in isolated areas. By mid-year the number of refugees flooding the camps in Southeast Asia had reached over 300,000, amidst reports that untold additional numbers had died at sea. While a majority continued to be of Chinese extraction, increasing numbers were native Vietnamese disillusioned with the revolution. State Secretary Nguyen Co Thach provided some insight into the scope of the problem, predicting that the exodus might continue for another two years and that the total number wishing to leave the country for various reasons could reach up to three million.[107]

The refugee conference held in Geneva in July seemed to promise an alleviation of the problem. Two days of negotiations produced a tacit agreement between the major parties involved to bring order to the situation. Vietnam agreed to enforce a temporary moratorium on emigration while Hanoi was able to elicit an agreement for an expanded UN program of "orderly departures" through direct and legel migration channels. Several countries (including the United

States, which agreed to accept 14,000 a month in 1979) agreed to increase their refugee quotas, while others such as Japan consented to finance the transportation costs.

For the time being, the conference had reduced the scope of the problem. By August the refugee flow had slowed to a trickle and the number of refugees in camps in Malaysia, Indonesia, and the Philippines began to decline.[108] Yet a final solution seemed elusive. If official projections of a future outflow of an additional two or three million is accurate, the burden of Indochinese refugees (for increasing numbers are likely to come from Cambodia and Laos), not only in Southeast Asia but around the world, is likely to increase. As the six-month moratorium came to an end in the spring of 1980, no solution appeared in sight.

Mass emigration was only one statistical indication of a revolution in serious trouble. The outward manifestations are primarily economic. The fact is, statistical indications are that the Five-Year Plan has been virtually scrapped. The Plan had envisaged an annual growth rate of approximately fifteen percent. That figure has never been remotely approached, dropping from nine percent in 1976 to less than two percent a year later. Since 1978 there has been virtually no progress at all. The problem has been exacerbated by a decline in exports and a drop in foreign assistance. Coal production, bedeviled with structural problems and the flight of ethnic Chinese, has been declining. Off the coast, exploratory teams have been finding a number of dry wells. The aftereffects of the Cambodian invasion were damaged as several major aid suppliers outside the socialist bloc cancelled assistance projects. The American trade embargo is still in existence and Washington has warned that unless Vietnamese troops are removed from Cambodia and Hanoi adopts a policy of greater distance from the Soviet Union, prospects for normalization are more remote than ever. Moscow has stepped up its own assistance in an effort to make up the difference, but in light of the current state of the Vietnamese economy (and heavy Soviet obligations elsewhere), the immediate prospects are not bright.

From a humanitarian standpoint, the most tragic aspect of the problem is its effect on the standard of the living for the average Vietnamese. Bad weather and peasant resistance to collectivization and grain purchases have continued to plague the agricultural sector and created a continuing shortage in grain production. The 1979 food deficit was estimated at 2.4 million tons of grain. Part of this was compensated from CEMA, but Vietnam was still left with a deficit of 500,000 tons. The inevitable result was more food rationing. Consumption was down to an average of about thirteen kilograms of food per person, half in rice and the remainder in potatoes, cassava, and wheat. Virtually all refugee accounts mention hunger as one of the major sources of dissatisfaction in Vietnam.[109] The problem is repeated in the case of other commodities. In officially approved state shops the shelves are virtually bare of goods. Often they are available on the black market (particularly in Ho Chi Minh City, where it flourishes at a rate parallel with the height of the American presence in Saigon), but at outrageously high prices.

The regime has belatedly made an effort to deal with the problem. After several attempts to stamp out black market activities, it has now decided to tolerate them, albeit with obvious reluctance. It has adopted new regulations to increase food production, raising the official purchasing price for rice, easing restrictions on the private raising of livestock and food, encouraging state farms and collectives to produce items not included in the plan with excess raw materials, and private farmers to produce more food and set their own prices, and instructing collective organizations to provide for wages on the basis of amount of work produced, in order to provide increased incentives.[110] Yet peasants are still reluctant to sell their produce to the state purchasing organization, particularly in the fertile Mekong Delta.

Despite such burgeoning problems, the government has not backed away from its program of collectivization in the Southern countryside. Recent statistics claim that by the end of 1979 collectivization was "virtually completed" in the Central provinces, with 83 percent of the farm families enrolled in either 1,114 full collectives or 1,500 production collectives. Comparable results had been achieved in the Central Highlands, where 74 percent of the peasants were collectively working on 66 percent of the total of cultivable land. There was less progress in the Southern provinces, where 12,000 production collectives had been established, but only half had "worked with collectivized production materials." And there were only 274 collectives in the area, the majority in Song Be and Tien Giang. One source admitted that the program "has encountered numerous difficulties" in the Mekong Delta, where private landowning peasants constituted the majority of the rural population. The regime's answer, as indicated in Nhan Dan, has been to advise cadres to be positive and urgent but steady, to work without hesitation but not in a hasty and haphazard manner, and to follow the path of voluntarism and mutual benefit, while avoiding coercion and threats.[111]

The regime also continued to place major emphasis on the effort to resettle the population into heretofore underdeveloped areas. Government statistics indicate that the program has had some success. By the end of 1978, 82 NEAs had been constructed in the South, with over 1.3 million members, and some 350,000 hectares of land had been reclaimed. According to Vice Prime Minister Le Thanh Nghi, however, that figure was well below the target set by the Five-Year Plan, and a major campaign was instituted to mobilize thousands of youths to work on the NEAs. Others were sent to cooperate with army units to build combat villages near the Cambodian border, to work on flood control projects, or on state farms. One government source reported that three million young people had volunteered to join the movement in one form or another. Yet here, too, the regime has run into difficulties. Articles in the official press have complained that many youths have failed to respond to the campaign and continue to engage in an unhealthy life style.

The serious deterioration in the economic situation places an additional strain on the social fabric of the country and on the morale of the population. The high level of emigration is only one manifestation. Press reports indicate that discontent with general conditions is prevalent among wide sectors of the population. There are signs of unrest in several areas in the South, particularly in regions inhabited by the sects, the mountain minorities, and Catholics, and there have been rumors of the formation of anti-communist organizations in preparation for an armed uprising against the regime. Several showtrials of

Buddhist bonzes have taken place in the South, and government prosecutors charge that prominent members of the Buddhist Church hierarchy have plotted against the regime.[112]

One of the least explored yet apparently most serious areas of dissatisfaction is among mountain tribesmen in the Central Highlands. Over the years the DRV had some success in persuading tribal groups in the North to switch from nomadic life to sedentary agriculture. That process is now underway in the South where, according to official statistics, 260,000 of the total of 800,000 tribal peoples in the region are in the process of shifting to settled farming. There is evidence, however, that the campaign has encountered stiff resistance. An additional source of unrest may also result from the program of settling lowland Vietnamese in upland areas traditionally reserved to the national minorities. Despite the contention in one official report that tribal compatriots have "happily welcomed" hundreds of thousands of Vietnamese to the mountains, another concedes that there have been serious disturbances in minority areas. The most prominent area of dissidence is reportedly among the Rhadé and Jarai peoples in the heart of the Central Highlands, where the anti-government tribal movement called FULRO (Front Uni pour la Liberation des Races Opprimés), originally formed to resist encroachments by the Saigon regime, had been revived. According to one source, this area is currently more dangerous for lowlanders to travel than Cambodia. Responding to such difficulties, one official source complains of "temporary difficulties and shortcomings of our cadres in implementing some policies in order to divide the fraternal peoples of various nationalities in our country and to disturb our Party's policy toward the nationalities."[113]

The regime's troubles with the mountain minorities are apparently not limited to the South. Concern over the loyalty of minority tribesmen in the Northern border regions adjacent to China led the regime recently to remove two of its most celebrated minority leaders, Chu Van Tan and Le Quang Ba, from positions of government and Party authority. An official source stated that while there was no indication of treasonous activities on the part of these elderly statesmen of the revolution, the Party leadership feared that they might be used by the Chinese to set up an anti-Vietnamese front among tribal groups along the border. According to the defector Hoang Van Hoan, after the close of the war in the South, there was considerable concern in Hanoi over the loyalty of border minorities who might be lured by the higher degree of prosperity among their kin north of the frontier. Accordingly, thousands were resettled to remote areas, while cadres who disagreed with the policy were punished or removed from positions of authority. While official sources claim that the minority peoples demonstrated their loyalty to the fatherland during the 1979 war with China, there may have been some instances of disaffection. Hanoi's White Paper did admit that Chinese provocateurs had attempted to set up a "mountaineer division" to be used against the PAVN in case of war, and there have been reports that some local residents sided with the Chinese during the recent invasion.[114]

As noted earlier, the problem has spilled over into neighboring Laos. When the central government in Vientiane has been stolidly pro-Hanoi since 1975, and has echoed Vietnamese criticism of Peking, Chinese agents have reportedly been working among the Meo and other tribal groups in the mountainous region in the North. Recently Hanoi charged that China had set up a "Meo Kingdom" near the border with the aid of Vang Pao, the Meo general who had fought with American support against the communist Pathet Lao in earlier years. In retaliation, the Laotian government demanded the removal of all Chinese laborers working on road projects in Northern Laos and a reduction in the staff of the Chinese Embassy. Some sources indicate that Vientiane's pro-Hanoi stance has not been popular among all elements in the LPRP. One defector claims that 90 percent of the Party members resent the continuing presence of Vietnamese troops and advisers in the country, and at least one high-ranking Party member has fled to China.[115]

It would have been surprising if the turmoil within Vietnamese society had not had repercussions on the vaunted unity of the Party leadership itself. For over a generation the VWP was one of the most monolithic parties within the entire communist movement. Between its founding in 1930 and the end of the war in 1975 there were virtually no cases of prominent defections to the enemy. There were internal disagreements during the generation of struggle to seize power in Vietnam, of course, and some may have been bitter and prolonged. And there may well have been identifiable factions favoring certain policies, although their existence and precise membership have never been established with certainty. But the inner tension was contained within the Party and apparently did not seriously hamper the making of policy or the Leninist tradition of democratic centralism. Since the end of the war, however, controversy has begun to erupt in public. The first sign appeared at the Fourth Party Congress in 1976 when a number of veteran communists, including Politburo member Hoang Van Hoan, were removed from their posts. While the reasons for the shakeup were not announced (some outside observers speculated at the time that Hoang Van Hoan had simply stepped down because of age), by the summer of 1978, when editorials in Nhan Dan reported serious discord within the leadership and predicted future defections to the enemy, it became clear that the problem was serious. In the summer of 1979 Hoang Van Hoan, ostensibly on a trip to East Berlin for medical treatment, defected at the airport in Karachi and later surfaced in Peking. At a press conference held shortly afterward he launched a bitter attack on Le Duan, claiming that since the death of Ho Chi Minh in 1969 Duan had assumed dictatorial control over the Party, purged it of those who disagreed with him, and destroyed the tradition of collective leadership that had existed for decades under the benign guidance of Uncle Ho.[116] According to Hoan, Le Duan's "Stalinist" methods had alienated many within the leadership, but that through his control of the public security apparatus he had been able to prevent the opposition from organizing or breaking out into the open.

Hoan's comments about dissension within the Party should obviously be treated with circumspection. It is noteworthy that in discussing disagreements within the Party he has avoided specifics, and emphasized the issue of Party democracy rather than domestic or foreign policy. On the other hand he has been openly critical of the anti-Peking stance adopted by the VCP under Le Duan's guidance, and it is likely that this was a major issue leading to his defection. Like several of his purged colleagues, Hoan had a reputation of sympathy for China, and may have been a victim of Hanoi's shift toward Moscow in the mid-1970s.

Hoan's defection has not ended the turmoil within the Party leadership. A _Nhan Dan_ editorial in November 1979 complained that "certain people . . .have shown doubts or vacillation in their feelings and actions. Some even stand the matter on its head [an apparent reference to the Vietnamese occupation of Cambodia: author]." Another editorial in the same newspaper the following January remarked that "some people" had "attacked the line and policies of the Party and its leaders" in private.[117] Then, in early 1980, there was a major realignment of the cabinet, with Vo Nguyan Giap replaced by Van Tien Dung as Minister of National Defense, Nguyen Duy Trinh by Nguyen Co Thach as Minister of Foreign Affairs, and Pham Hung taking the place of Tran Quoc Hoan as Minister of the Interior. The Central Party Military Committee has reportedly been reorganized, with Le Duan replacing Giap as chairman. There have been persistent rumors that either Giap, Le Duan, or Pham Van Dong will be promoted to the prestigious post of chairman of the State Council, left vacant since the death of Ho Chi Minh. Some of these changes can be ascribed to the natural process of youth replacing age. Both Giap and Nguyen Duy Trinh have reportedly been ill and rumored for retirement for years. But many of the changes seem designed to strengthen Le Duan's control over the Party and the security apparatus. A number of the new appointees, including Van Tien Dung and Pham Hung, are considered to be close to Duan. Further changes are anticipated at a forthcoming session of the National Assembly, which may also approve the new Constitution which has been under discussion for three years, and the aim of which is to provide a charter for the transition of the entire country to socialism.[118]

Similar changes are taking place within the Party, which is now undergoing a period of rectification to purge the organization of undesirable elements. After victory in the South, a number of new members were added, raising the total membership to well over one million. According to official sources, many are now considered incompetent, corrupt, lazy, or to carry the "noxious influence of Maoism." It has been rumored that up to one-half the total membership might be dismissed. Official reports emphasize that the stress in determining an individual's status will be placed on behavior and attitude, not on class background.[119]

It is clear that Vietnam is currently undergoing a period of serious internal turmoil. Some of this may be ascribed to the policies of the Party leadership which has characteristically not backed away from challenge, but rushed to meet it head on. There is a stubborn, determined, almost foolhardy quality about the communist leadership in Vietnam which was frequently demonstrated during the war in the South and is now openly displayed in its policies during the postwar period. The time may yet come when the revolutionary hubris of the Party leads it into a serious miscalculation, either in terms of the mood of the population as a whole or its capacity to act effectively beyond its frontiers. Through reports by refugees and foreign observers comes the feeling that the mood of the Vietnamese people is sullen, if not mutinous.

Still, it would be premature at this stage to judge the Vietnamese revolution as a failure. All revolutions have gone through a period of serious travail and many, including those in Russia and China, have at various times been popularly slated for demise. The Vietnamese people are talented, industrious, and, when the occasion demands, incredibly patient. The Party itself is experienced and determined, and blessed with a long tradition of discipline, sacrifice, and loyalty. This is not the first time that Le Duan and his colleagues have been confronted with problems that seem virtually insurmountable. On previous occasions, through persistence, astuteness, and good fortune, they have managed to survive and triumph.

They are in sore need of such qualities today. Despite the determination and optimism that consistently emanates from Hanoi, the prospects for the immediate future are not bright. The economic situation continues to deteriorate. The occupation of Cambodia shows no signs of coming to an end. Rivalry with Peking and the threat of a new invasion provides an ominous counterpoint from the North. Much, of course, depends on the nature of the future policies of the regime itself. Will it temper its determination to achieve a rapid transition to socialism under the accumulated pressures of economic difficulties and popular discontent? What are Hanoi's intentions in foreign affairs? Will it be content to maintain a hammerlock on Laos and Cambodia, or will it be tempted to promote insurgency movements elsewhere in the region? While Vietnam has not yet been transformed into an "Asian Cuba" serving as the proxy for Soviet objectives in the Third World, there are signs that such a metamorphosis may take place in the future. Even under present conditions the regime has not hesitated to risk greater foreign involvement by its military operations inside Thailand, leading China to voice ominous warnings of possible consequences. The answers to such questions will probably depend on the regime's success in resolving its economic difficulties, and, perhaps even more, on the general trend of events in the region and the world as a whole. If the current signs of global instability spread to Southeast Asia, Hanoi may well be tempted to add its own considerable weight on the side of revolutions abroad. If such is the case, the likelihood of renewed Great Power conflict in the region will be considerably heightened.

Under such circumstances, American policies in the area have come under serious scrutiny and criticism. Several observers have contended that the Carter Administration should have pursued its strategy of normalizing relations with Hanoi even in the face of the refugee issue, the threat with Moscow, and the invasion of Cambodia, on the assumption that a conciliatory policy in Washington might have encouraged moderate forces within the Vietnamese Party leadership. One high official in Hanoi has implicitly supported the contention by declaring that Vietnam would be less pro-Soviet if the United States provided a diplomatic counterweight against China.[120] Current policies in Washington, in this view, have only served to force Hanoi into the arms of the Soviet Union.

Unfortunately, the issue is not that simple. In the first place, the Vietnam issue lies at the juncture of three major and sometimes conflicting forces in American foreign policy - those of morality, of domestic politics, and of realpolitik. Under present conditions, when American public attitudes toward Vietnam have hardened and opinions on foreign policy in general have shifted sharply to the right, it would be very difficult for the Carter Administration, beset by weakness and lack of public support, to undertake a serious initiative to resolve differences with Hanoi, even if real foreign policy advantages might be the result.

Moreover, it is not certain that decisions reached in Washington could exert a meaningful influence on the course of policy in Hanoi. It may well be true that with a more conciliatory attitude from the United States, Vietnam would not have joined CEMA. It is highly doubtful, however, that American initiatives could have significantly altered the course of Vietnamese internal policy, or affected Hanoi's decision to overthrow the Pol Pot regime. At the present juncture, Hanoi's primary domestic objective is to achieve a rapid and thorough transition to a fully socialist society. In foreign affairs, its major requirements are dominance throughout Indochina and protection against the renewed threat from a hostile China determined to limit Soviet influence along its Southern frontier. Under these circumstances, there is little that Washington can do to affect policies or change minds in Hanoi. It can hardly approve internal policies which are repugnant to American moral principles and which have apparently given birth to serious discontent even within Vietnam itself. It can hardly provide Hanoi with a meaningful counterbalance against China at a time when the American relationship with Peking is considered crucially necessary to the containment of the Soviet threat on a global scale. The fact is, for the time being, the current Party leadership in Vietnam is ideologically and emotionally locked into a rigid Marxist-Leninist view of social change and a foreign policy which is basically linked to that of the Soviet Union. It is capable of tactical shifts for the purpose of immediate advantage. It is not likely to be susceptible to major policy shifts of the kind ardently desired by Washington - and Peking.

Under such conditions, the Carter Administration has relatively little room to maneuver. Normalization of diplomatic and economic relations might serve to reduce the long legacy of hostility between Washington and Hanoi, and that is ardently to be desired. But it would not deter the Party leadership from undertaking policies which are currently considered vital to its national interests. The question that remains is whether or not it is preferable to withhold such relations until such time as they can be used as a bargaining counter to achieve a more meaningful shift in Vietnamese policies. Washington has apparently concluded that for the moment there is little that it can do to affect the situation in Vietnam and has decided to wait, for several years if necessary, for the departure of Le Duan and the emergence of a more flexible leadership in Hanoi. While there are no current signs that such an adjustment is actually taking place, it should not be ruled out for the future. The rapid shifts in power in Peking in recent years have demonstrated that even communist parties are susceptible to change under the pressure of momentous decisions. In Vietnam today, the Party leadership is beset with serious problems, many of its own making. Statements in the official press show clearly that a moderate opposition does exist within the Party leadership, and certainly in society as a whole. The United States should do what it can to influence the nature of that ongoing debate. It should attempt to encourage the emergence of moderate social forces within the Vietnamese revolution. It should do its part to promote the resolution of the issues which currently divide Hanoi and Peking and thus serve as a source of potential instability throughout the entire region. And it should also be a primary objective of American policy to strengthen the capacity of all the nations in the area, including Vietnam, to preserve their independence and freedom from outside domination, whatever the source. Given the harsh and uncompromising forces presently at work within the region and the exigencies of Cold War politics, this will not be an easy task. The forces released by social revolution do not abate over a period of months, or even years. The ability of the United States to influence, for good or ill, the course of events in the region has seriously declined since the withdrawal of American military forces from South Vietnam. Yet it should persist, for the reduction of the sources of tension and conflict in Southeast Asia is in the national interest, not only of the United States, but of Vietnam and the other states in the region, and the world as a whole.

[1] Lenin's most detailed exposition of his views came in The State and Revolution, written on the eve of the Bolshevik seizure of power in 1917. Marx and Engels had dealt with the issue of the Dictatorship of the Proletariat, but only in general terms.

[2] Mao Tse-tung, On New Democracy, (London: Lawrence & Wishart, 1954), Vol. 3.

[3] Technically speaking, the ICP claimed that its own approach relied to a greater degree than its Chinese counterpart on the need for a general uprising in the cities to supplement the revolutionary takeover in rural areas. In general, however, Vietnamese strategy after 1941 resembled the Maoist doctrine of people's war in most respects. For a more detailed discussion of this issue, see my The Communist Road to Power in Vietnam (Westview Press, forthcoming).

[4] A Vietnamese-language version of Truong Chinh's Political Report to the Congress is located in Communist Vietnamese Publications, reel 2, number 60. This source is a microfilm collection of translated communist documents issued by the Library of Congress.

[5] For a recent analysis of the economic performance of the DRV, see Nguyen Tien Hung, Economic Development of Socialist Vietnam, 1955-1980 (New York: Praeger, 1977).

[6] South Viet Nam National Front for Liberation: Documents (Saigon: Giai Phong Publishing House, 1968).

[7] This plan was openly discussed in a number of captured documents. In effect, the coalition regime played the role of preparing for the transition from the first to the second stage of the revolution.

[8] This decision is discussed in General Van Tien Dung's Our Great Spring Victory (New York and London: Monthly Review Press, 1977), p. 242.

[9] Two journalistic accounts of the fall of Saigon are Tiziano Terzani, Giai Phong: The Fall and Liberation of Saigon (New York: St. Martin's Press, 1976), and Denis Warner, Not With Guns Alone (London: Hutchinson, 1977).

[10] Civilian officials of the GVN were considered by the new regime as the worst enemy because they had "directly and enthusiastically participated in the population control apparatus." See Saigon Giai Phong (Liberated Saigon), November 8, 1975. For a discussion of the standards used to determine the degree of guilt, see Foreign Broadcast Information Service, Volume IV (Asia and the Pacific), January 29, 1976. Hereafter this source will be cited as FBIS. All sources cited are in Volume IV.

[11] Che Viet Tan, "Redistribute labor and population, develop our people's abundant labor and strength in national construction," in Tap Chi Cong San (Communist Review), February 1977, in FBIS, March 30, 1977.

[12] Hoang Ngoc, "General education in South Vietnam," in Hoc Tap (Study), December 1976.

[13] Che Viet Tan, "Redistribute . . . ."

[14] For a brief discussion, see Le Duan, The Vietnamese Revolution: Fundamental Problems and Essential Tasks (New York: International Publishers, 1971), p. 93.

[15] Nhan Dan (the People), November 20, 1975.

[16] See the article on the campaign against the "barbed wire king" in Nhan Dan, September 18, 1975.

[17] For the regulations, see Nguyen Tien Hung, Economic Development . . . , appendix, pp. 167-170.

[18] Nguyen Khac Vien, interview in Rinascita, April 30, 1976.

[19] Editorial in Hoc Tap, April 1976, as translated in Joint Publications Research Service (JPRS) 67,373, Translations on North Vietnam 1806. Unless otherwise indicated, journalistic references used in this study are from this source.

[20] Ho Liem, "A number of matters concerning the social revolution in our country in the new stage," Hoc Tap, November 1975.

[21] Ibid.

[22] Chinh's speech appears in FBIS, December 11, 1975. For an additional description of the regime's plans, see the comments by Mme. Nguyen Thi Binh in the New York Times, March 7, 1976.

[23] Nguyen Khac Vien, interview in Rinascita, April 30, 1976.

[24] For a citation to this effect, see footnote 56, below.

[25] The series of articles began on November 27, 1975.

[26] Ibid., citing Vladimir Lenin, The Immediate Task of the Soviet Administration.

[27] At this time, Saigon was renamed Ho Chi Minh City. The new government included several native South Vietnamese among its ranks, including Huynh Tan Phat (formerly chairman of the PRC) as vice president. According to a news report, twenty percent of the members of the Assembly were peasants, eighteen percent were intellectuals, ten percent were soldiers, nine percent were political officials, and 1.6 percent were workers. One quarter were women. See the New York Times, June 25, 1976.

[28] Information on the Five-Year Plan is located in the materials on the Fourth Party Congress, in FBIS, Vol. IV, No. 247, supplement 48.

[29] Le Duan, The Vietnamese Revolution . . . , p. 120. The statistics are from Nghien Cuu Kinh Te (Economic Research), November-December 1975. The standard reason given for managerial weaknesses in the Party is that it has traditionally been composed primarily of peasants, rather than workers or the petty bourgeoisie.

[30] Che Viet Tan, "Redistribute . . . ."

[31] Cong Tac Ke Hoach (Planning Work), October 1975, pp. 46-49.

[32] Nguyen Khac Vien, interview in Rinascita, April 30, 1976.

[33] Le Duan's Political Report at the Fourth Party Congress, Volume II, p. 60.

[34] Fox Butterfield, "Peking-Hanoi talks marked by coolness," in New York Times, August 15, 1975. According to this source, Teng Hsiao-p'ing did not see Deputy Prime Minister Le Thanh Nghi during the latter's visit, a reflection of Peking's irritation at Hanoi's lack of gratitude for Chinese assistance during the war. This was later confirmed by China. See Beijing Review, September 7, 1979, p. 25.

[35] Duan's statement is in his Political Report to the Congress. See FBIS, Vol. IV, No. 247, supplement 48, Vol. II.

[36] Soviet universalism was expressed in the formation of the Comintern in 1919, and in support for revolts in Central Europe at the end of World War I. China was more cautious, but did express support for people's wars in the Third World, as expressed in Liu Shao-ch'i's famous speech at the 1949 Trade Union Congress held in Peking.

[37] For example, see the article by Hoang Tung, editor of Nhan Dan, in the February 1977 issue of Tap Chi Cong San.

[38] Hanoi, VNA in English, June 25, 1976.

[39] The absence of native Lao and Khmer in the early years of the movement is well established in materials contained in the archives of the old Ministry of Colonies in Paris.

[40] Hanoi, VNA in English, April 7, 1978.

[41] This and the above quote are located in the United States Department of State, Working Paper on North Viet-Nam's Role in the War in South Viet-Nam (Washington, D.C., 1968), Appendix Item number 1, p. 2-2, entitled "Remarks on the official appearance of the Vietnamese Workers' Party."

[42] This charge is contained in The Truth about Viet Nam - China Relations over the Last 30 Years (Hanoi: Ministry of Foreign Affairs, 1979), pp. 12-16.

[43] Ibid., p. 28.

[44] Hoan has long been rumored to be a member of an alleged pro-Chinese faction within the Politburo. Le Duan, on the other hand, is considered to be pro-Soviet.

[45] Black Paper: Facts and Evidences of the Acts of Aggression and Annexation of Vietnam against Kampuchea (Phnom Penh: Ministry of Foreign Affairs, 1978), pp. 23-25.

[46] The Vietnamese now claim that Peking sponsored this conference in order to establish Chinese dominance over the revolutionary movement in Indochina. White Paper, p. 33. The official record of the conference is located in Vietnam Documents and Research Notes (Saigon: U.S. Mission), Document number 80 (June 1970). Hereafter this source will be cited as VDRN.

[47] VDRN, Document number 88, cites examples of such tensions.

[48] An English translation of Brevie's original note is located in FBIS, April 7, 1978. Also see Far Eastern Economic Review, February 3, 1978. Hereafter FEER.

[49] Black Paper, pp. 3-14.

[50] R. P. Paringaux, "The conflict between Vietnam and Cambodia," in Le Monde, March 30, 1978, as cited in JPRS 71:017, Translations on Vietnam 2031. This source contains a useful summary of the history of the KCP.

[51] For a running analysis of Sino-Laotian relations, see FEER, June 16, 1978; September 1, 1978; Feburary 23, 1979; April 6, 1979.

[52] Interview with Nguyen Duy Trinh in Hanoi, VNA, July 5, 1976.

[53] Ibid.

[54] Nguyen Van Tran, "Continue to struggle to eliminate the comprador bourgeoisie and those who speculate, hoard and monopolize the market at present," in Hoc Tap, September 1976.

[55] Nhan Dan, November 2, 1975.

[56] For example, see the article in Nguoi Xay Dung (the Builder), November 1978. Refugee accounts, however, often note that there was frequent favoritism toward revolutionary families, and discrimination against those with a middle class background. For one such comment, see Bruce Grant, The Boat People: An 'Age' Investigation (Harmondsworth: Penguin, 1979), p. 103.

[57] See the article by Siegfried Kogelfranz, "Waiting for the fruits of victory," in Der Spiegel, March 13, 1978, in JPRS 70,768. Translations on Vietnam 2017. According to this source, the standard reply to the question was that on the average about three percent had left the new settlements. Some observers speculated that the true figure was nearer to one-half.

[58] Ibid., gives one example.

[59] Nhan Dan, August 4, 1977.

[60] Nhan Dan, March 24, 1978.

[61] According to the June 1978 issue of Tap Chi Cong San, only one-fifth of the goods uncovered had been declared.

[62] FBIS, April 6, 1978, has the official announcement. With a few weeks the regime was complaining of the reappearance of open air markets. See Tin Sang, June 17, 1978. Time, September 4, 1978, claims that private markets were open during the evening hours, even in Hanoi.

[63] See the article by Do Muoi in Tap Chi Cong San, May 1978. One government official said that in six months, 16,000 petty bourgeois traders had shifted to handicrafts, animal husbandry, or the NEAs. See AFP report, FBIS, September 29, 1978. Hanoi, VNA, November 9, 1978, claimed that 54 percent of all small industry in Ho Chi Minh City had been placed under collective ownership.

[64] Nhan Dan editorial, April 1, 1978. A few days later, Nhan Dan returned to the attack and noted that some Party members "leaned to the right" in their political orientation. See Nhan Dan, April 13, 1978.

[65] Nhan Dan, January 9, 1979. For a detailed description of production collectives and work exchange teams, see Nhan Dan, June 27-28, 1978.

[66] Speech by Vo Chi Cong, cited in JPRS 71,904, Translations on Vietnam 2063.

[67] These statistics are from Nhan Dan, June 27-28, 1978.

[68] Laszlo Bogos, "The transformation of South Vietnam," Magyar Hirlap, March 9-11, 1978, cited in JPRS 71,017, Translations on Vietnam 2027.

[69] Nong Nghiep (Agriculture), October 20, 1979. The speech by Vo Chi Cong cited above is in Hanoi Domestic Service, August 26, 1978.

[70] Nhan Dan, August 4, 1978.

[71] Two views are in FEER, June 16, 1978, and Bruce Grant, The Boat People, pp. 87, 109.

[72] Washington Post, May 29, 1978. Grant, p. 112, cites Chinese sources that 160,000 had fled to China by mid-June. Vietnamese sources put the figure at 140,000.

[73] Beijing Review, March 30, 1979. Apparently many ethnic Chinese did not choose to apply for Vietnamese citizenship, perhaps as a means of avoiding the draft.

[74] Such statements are located in Pham Van Dong's interview in AFP, September 3, 1978, and White Paper, pp. 43-45, and The Truth . . . , pp. 43-45.

[75] See, for example, Grant, pp. 94-96, 104.

[76] Jay Matthews, "Peking impedes flight of Chinese from Vietnam," in Washington Post, July 14, 1978; James Sterba, "Some Vietnamese ethnic Chinese find life hard in China," in New York Times, September 11, 1979.

[77] A description of the process is located in FEER, December 22, 1978. The government would take half, while the remainder was used to defrat costs for the middleman. See Henry Kamm, "Hanoi denies it is fostering exodus," in New York Times, December 12, 1978. Some refugee sources say the program was run by Nguyen Van Linh and had been patterned after the Cuban example.

[78] Nhan Dan, November 25, 1978.

[79] FEER, August 18, 1978.

[80] Thach's quote is in Henry Kamm, "Key topic in Vietnam: likelihood of a Chinese attack," in New York Times, August 17, 1979.

[81] The full text is in New Times (Moscow), November 1978, pp. 6-7. There were rumors of the existence of a secret military protocol.

[82] AFP, November 4, 1978.

[83] Henry Kamm, "Key topic . . . ," New York Times, August 17, 1979.

[84] Beijing Review, May 25, 1979, citing speech by Han Nien-long at negotiating session on May 12, 1979. Also see Vietnam News Bulletin, April 10, 1979, entitled "Memorandum on Chinese provocations and territorial encroachments upon Vietnamese territory."

[85] FEER, March 16, 1979. For a discussion on the differences, see Beijing Review, May 25, 1979, and Vietnam News Bulletin, April 10, 1979, "Memorandum on . . . ."

[86] FEER, "Pouring trouble on oily waters," September 28, 1979.

[87] For a discussion, see Beijing Review, February 18, 1980, "Chinese indisputable sovereignty over the Xisha and Nansha islands."

[88] Beijing Review, August 24, 1979. An English translation of Pham Van Dong's letter, and a facsimile of the Vietnamese original, is in Ibid., May 25, 1979. For the Vietnamese claim, see The New York Times, September 29, 1979.

[89] China claims Pham Van Dong admitted that Hanoi had to appear to recognize China's claims because of the wartime situation. See Ibid., August 24, 1979.

[90] Cited in FBIS, January 17, 1978.

[91] Two of the rising figures were generals Hoang Cam, in charge of Cambodian operation, and Le Trong Tan, Van Tien Dung's deputy during the Ho Chi Minh campaign.

[92] "The revolution is dead," in Le Monde, October 24, 1978.

[93] For the program, see New York Times, December 4, 1978.

[94] Don Oberdorfer, "Vietnam deep into its third war," in Washington Post, August 6, 1978. Also see William Safire's article entitled "Indochina War II," in New York Times, January 5, 1979.

[95] FEER, September 15, 1978.

[96] Seymour Hersh, "Hanoi asserts ties with U.S. were set," in New York Times, August 7, 1979.

[97] Daniel Tretiak, "China's Vietnam War and its Consequences," China Quarterly, (December 1979), p. 749.

[98] A military analysis of the war is located in Harlan W. Jencks, "China's 'punitive' war on Vietnam: A military assessment," Asian Survey (August 1979).

[99] For a text of the Soviet declaration, see New York Times, February 20, 1979. For the rumors of the Sino-Soviet agreement, see Tretiak, p. 750.

[100] Trenchant comments on the performance of the PLA and PAVN can be found in the articles by Drew Middleton in the New York Times. See esp. "How Chinese performed," March 6, 1979.

[101] Beijing Review, May 4, 1979.

[102] Military experts feel that the best route in the future would be through Laos and into the Haiphong-Hanoi axis. See FEER July 20, 1979. But China may feel that its best strategy would be to mobilize international opinion against the SRV and let internal tensions work at the Party leadership in Hanoi. See Fox Butterfield, "China stands firm amid growing crises," New York Times, January 5, 1980.

[103] FEER, January 4, 1980.

[104] FEER, July 6, 1979.

[105] FEER, March 30, 1980.

[106] Interview with Hoang Tung in AFP, September 7, 1978.

[107] FEER, August 24, 1979.

[108] According to the United Nations High Commissioner on Refugees, the total number of refugees in Asian camps in June 1980 was slightly under 100,000. This, however, did not include several hundred thousand Cambodians in Thailand. New York Times, June 12, 1980.

109 For example, see Barry Wain, "South Vietnamese experience the pains of integration into a communist state," in Wall Street Journal, June 6, 1980.

110 For example, see the reference to the resolution of the Sixth Plenum of the Central Committee held in October 1979 in the speech by Agricultural Minister Nguyen Ngoc Trieu quoted in Nhan Dan, November 14-15, 1979.

111 Hanoi Domestic Service in Vietnamese, April 29, 1980.

112 For one such report see Jong Kong, the account of the so-called National Vietnam Action Movement in JPRS 75,456, Translations on Vietnam 2180. Among Buddhist leaders prominent in the anti-Saigon movement before the comminist takeover, several have been placed under arrest. Thich Thien Minh reportedly died in prison, while Tri Quang has been living under house arrest.

113 FEER, June 22, 1979.

114 For a reference to Vietnamese fears, see FEER, June 9, 1978.

115 FEER, August 24, 1979. For a Chinese view, cf. Beijing Review, June 22, 1979.

116 For Hoang Van Hoan's interview, see Beijing Review, August 17 and September 7, 1979.

117 Cited in Beijing Review, February 18, 1980.

118 For a discussion of the new Constitution, see FBIS, February 7, 1978, and JPRS 75,213, Translations on Vietnam 2173. A copy of the draft constitution was published as a supplement to FBIS, Vol. IV, supplement 027, no. 185, September 21, 1979.

119 According to FEER, February 18, 1980, the purge was initiated at a meeting of the Politburo in February 1979, followed by a Central Committee directive in May. The aim is to achieve a Party purified at the grass roots level by the end of 1980.

120 New York Times, August 17, 1979. Criticisms of American policy can be found in Bruce Grant, The Boat People, p. 200, and in FEER, February 2, 1979. A particularly insightful discussion is Jeffrey Race and William S. Turley, "The Third Indochina War," in Foreign Policy (Spring 1980), no. 38, pp. 92-116.